# THE PINNACLE OF LIFE

# ABOUT THE AUTHOR

Dr Derek Denton has spent decades in biomedical scientific research, with a primary interest in evolutionary biology. He is regarded as an international leader in investigation of instinctive behaviour, particularly that bearing upon the intake of fluids, minerals and food and the way changes of the body chemistry and hormones affect brain function.

Following publication of his book *The Hunger for Salt* in 1982, the New York Times described him as 'an Australian physician and scientist who is probably the world's foremost authority on the biology and behaviour of salt use'.

Professor Denton is a Foreign Medical Member of the Royal Swedish Academy of Sciences, an Honorary Foreign Member of the American Academy of Arts and Sciences and a Fellow of the Australian Academy of Sciences. He was first Vice-president of the International Union of Physiological Sciences, 1983–1989, and is a member of the Board of the Australian Ballet Foundation and *The Age* newspaper.

He is currently investigating behaviour of chimpanzees and gorillas in Equatorial Africa, and appetites of baboons at the Southwest Foundation for Medical Research in Texas, as well as continuing his studies on hormones and the brain at the Howard Florey Institute of Experimental Physiology and Medicine in Melbourne, Australia.

# THE PINNACLE
# OF LIFE

## Consciousness and Self-Awareness in Humans and Animals

Derek Denton

HarperSanFrancisco

*A Division of* HarperCollins*Publishers*

FIRST HARPERCOLLINS PAPERBACK EDITION PUBLISHED IN 1994

Library of Congress Cataloging-in-Publication Data
Denton, Derek A.
   The pinnacle of life : consciousness and self-awareness in humans
   and animals / Derek Denton — 1st HarperCollins pbk. ed.
   p. cm.
   Originally published: Sydney: Allyn & Unwin, 1993.
   Includes bibliographical references and index.
   ISBN 0–06–251124–6 (pbk: alk. paper)
   1. Consciousness.   2. Consciousness in animals.
   3. Self-perception.   4. Mind and Body.   I. Title.

BF311.D465   1994                                              94-5947
156'.3—dc20                                                        CIP

94 95 96 97 98 RRD (H) 10 9 8 7 6 5 4 3 2 1

This edition is printed on acid-free paper that meets the
American National Standards Institute Z39.48 Standard.

# Contents

*To R. Douglas Wright, Kenneth Myer and Alfred Conlon, who liked talking about things.*

# Acknowledgments

It is a great pleasure to thank the many people who have helped me during the writing of this book, with suggestions and discussions and the provision of references. However, needless to say, they have no responsibility for any errors of fact or interpretation.

Sir Andrew Huxley and Lady Huxley generously invited me to stay with them in the Master's Lodge at Trinity College, Cambridge, which allowed discussion, writing and access to wonderful library facilities there, and in Cambridge. At Cambridge, I was much indebted also to Professor Eric Handley, Professor of Greek, to Professor Anne Barton, Professor of English, to Ms Janet Huxley, and to Professor Geoffrey Lloyd, Master of Darwin College, for references. Professor Roger Short, of Monash University, kindly read a draft manuscript, and I am very grateful to him for comments and many references, and also to Mr Harold Stewart of Kyoto, Japan, for comments and references. I am also grateful to Lady Drysdale and Mr Harry Oppenheimer for references and the use of their libraries. Dr Alan Dixon and Dr Nick Mundy of the

Centre International de Recherche Medicale of Franceville, Gabon, read draft sections of the manuscript during the course of my sojourn there during our experimental work on chimpanzees and gorillas and they provided helpful comment.

Apart from the issues covered in the transcript, discussions at Ashton Wold with Dr Miriam Rothschild were catalytic of many ideas, as were discussions with Dr Roger Guillemin and I am most appreciative, as I am also to Robyn Williams, Patrick Gallagher, Robin Hughes, Elizabeth Cavendish, Margaret Scott and Frank Tait, who have all discussed aspects of the text with me. I am most grateful to Sir Evelyn and Lady de Rothschild and Mrs Joyce Miles, for hospitality at Lodsbridge Mill, Sussex, where much of the book was written. Ms Eira Parry has given me enormous help in the typing and editing of the manuscript, and her good humour and energy have been invaluable. Mr Sam Critchley, Ms Mary McBurnie, Mr Novel Uch and Mr Tony Shafton were most helpful with illustrative material.

# Permissions

I wish to thank the persons and/or publishers detailed below for the kind permission to quote from the works cited or to reproduce diagrams:

The Nobel foundation for passages from the lectures of Sir Winston Churchill, Nobel Laureate in Literature in 1953, Pablo Neruda, Nobel Laureate in Literature 1971 and Saul Bellow, Nobel Laureate in Literature in 1976; The Pontifica Academia Scientiarum for the passage from *Brain and Conscious Experience*, edited by J.C. Eccles and published by Springer Verlag, Heidelberg, being an audience with His Holiness Pope Paul VI and a lecture by Dr Wilder Penfield; Professor J.Z. Young and the Oxford University Press for passages from *Philosophy and the Brain*; Dr Roger Sperry of the California Institute of Technology for extracts from 'Mind–Brain Interaction', in *Neuroscience* 5, 195, 1980; Dr Allan Hobson of Harvard University for a passage from *The Dreaming Brain*, Basic Books Inc; Dr Geoffrey Lloyd, Master of Darwin College, Cambridge University, for a passage from *Aristotle—The Growth and Structure of his Thought*, Cambridge University Press; Random House, London, and the Estate of Marcel

Proust, for passages from *Remembrance of Things Past* by Marcel Proust, translated by T. Kilmartin, and published by Chatto and Windus; Thames & Hudson, London, for a passage from the book *Andre Malraux, Past, Present and Future, Conversations with E. Saures*; Dr Lewis Thomas, and Doubleday, New York, for a passage from *Living Philosophies*, edited by Clifton Fadiman, and for a passage from *The Medusa and the Snail*, Viking Press; S. Karger, Basle, for a passage from *Folio Primatologica* by Dr Geza Teleki; Dr E.O. Wilson of Harvard University for a passage from *Biophilia*, published by Harvard University Press; Methuen, London, for a passage from *King Solomon's Ring* by Konrad Lorenz; The Harry Frank Guggenheim Foundation for the photograph of Dr Donald Griffin by Fabian Bachrach; Dr Francine Patterson and The Gorilla Foundation for photographs of Koko taken by Ronald H. Cohn. The diagram of drawing ability following the division of the corpus callosum was reproduced from Michael Gazzaniga's book *The Social Brain*, copyright 1985 Basic Books Inc., by permission of Harper Collins; the photographs of Vicki are from the paper of Keith and Catherine Hayes, Proc.Amer. Phil.Soc. (95) 12, 1951, and *The Ape in Our House* by Catherine Hayes, published by Harper, New York. I would also like to thank Mr Graham Pizzey for permission to reproduce two of his photographs of bower birds, and Ms Christine Walsh for permission to reproduce the photographs of Benjamin and the mirror taken by Margaret Scott.

# Introduction

This book will pose and discuss many of the fascinating questions concerning consciousness in humans and animals. It is for both the layperson and the medical biologist who have in common a consuming curiosity and thirst for knowledge about the functions of the brain.

Experiments showing there is self-recognition in mirrors by the great apes indicate that they have crossed the threshold to self-awareness—it is me! In *The Pinnacle of Life* we will examine brain–mind functions in the ascent of the evolutionary tree to this pinnacle. But it is obvious that there is a gaping void between an ape examining otherwise-visually-inaccessible parts of its body with a mirror, or, with the aid of a mirror, fingering a mark painted on its forehead while it was anaesthetised, and the soliloquy of Hamlet. A part of the book looks into this void, and at some of the evolutionary forces that have shaped the human intellect, the character of society, and the concurrent emergence of artistic expression.

The viewpoint I will take is that consciousness, both perceptive and self-awareness, has arisen in the course of the ascent of life from the primaeval brine because it confers spectacular survival advantage. The ability to make the present congruent with the past, and to imagine future scenarios, carries vast dividends in the struggle for survival. Notions can be tested in the mind, not in nature, and the animal reduces the chances of being killed. Consciousness has been honed on the anvil of natural selection—an essentially Darwinian viewpoint, and one not involving any external intervention or other-worldly influences.

However, there are other viewpoints on the latter subject, as displayed in the course of debate—specifically with Sir John Eccles.

Whereas the preponderance of discussion of contemporary knowledge will centre on broad scientific analysis of brain function, the view espoused will be anything but an avowal that analysis is a domain peculiar to biomedical science—be it neurosurgery, comparative behaviour or any other of the many facets of neuroscience discussed. Self-evidently, the questions of consciousness and self-awareness have preoccupied poets, philosophers, writers, as well as natural scientists, for millennia.

For most of those who delight in the companion animals—dogs and cats—there would be little difficulty in persuading them that there is somebody home inside the skull. The creatures tend on occasions to make their needs and desires known. The tail-wagging and yelping can get results. It seems a level of communication exists. But in some eyes maybe they are just automata, endowed with highly complex programs according to the species, and they respond to stimuli. Given rewarding outcomes, some patterns become facilitated and dominant in their behaviour, and their demeanour changes with time—they learn.

However, quite novel situations do arise which provoke the notion that the creature has something of a mind, forms images and evaluates options. In the book there will be accounts of events at this level, as well as records of systematic inquiry. Accounts of individual or singular instances, even when made with detached objectivity by trained scientific minds, can be termed anecdotal—literally the narrative of an interesting incident or event. In scientific literature it often carries a lightweight or rather dismissive overtone. No doubt, sometimes such accounts are trivial and of no general significance, but there is no necessary great methodological gap between such knowledge arising from astute observation of chance behaviour of many species including companion animals, and that deriving, for example, from systematic recording of spontaneous behaviour in the wild of creatures such as the great apes.

It is evident in his book *The Expression of the Emotions in Man and Animals* the extent to which Charles Darwin was prepared to integrate the accounts of particular events recounted by his many naturalist friends and clinicians into the ideas he was advancing. Konrad Lorenz obviously drew a great deal from his observation of his companion animals in domestic circumstances as well as his systematic comparative studies of behaviour, termed 'ethology'. In interpreting animal behaviour, and in particular in avoiding projecting on to creatures elements of human motivation—so-called 'anthropomorphising'—Miriam Rothschild emphasises the need to be aware constantly of heightened sensory capacities in different animal species. Their endowment may be far superior to man in specific instances. Thus one can be misled in interpreting why an animal does something.

My own compelling interest in consciousness arises as an experimental physiologist investigating the mainsprings of behaviour. It is fascinating to watch the demeanour and direction of attention of an animal change rapidly as one deliberately, by unobstrusive experimental manoeuvre, alters the chemical composition of blood flowing through the brain or quickly changes the chemistry of the tissue fluid within the brain. It would seem the direction of attention, the relevance of environmental events, indeed the stream of consciousness of the creature, has been changed in a fascinating and quite reproducible fashion. The animal now wants something and may demonstrate its desire unambiguously.

However, whereas all manner of brain processes (electrical and turning on of expression of genes) have been demonstrated to change when one does something like this, how awareness actually alters remains a great mystery. With the brilliant new techniques of brain scanning or imaging in humans such as positron emission tomography (PET), extraordinary insight has come from studies where, indeed, there are no internal or external stimuli at all. Only the mind's eye need wander from one issue of attention to another, and thereupon different local areas of the brain light up with activity—the mind itself, the actual thoughts, determining shifts of the locale of heightened brain function. We have little idea how it works, any more than we know whether the buck fleeing from a cheetah and weaving in every way has any concept of its impending injury and doom. Or whether it is rather an automaton with a program of evasion in response to the visual stimulus—the configuration of a cheetah?

This book is derived from a series of radio broadcasts made for the Australian Broadcasting Commission's Science program at the invitation of Robyn Williams, the program's Director. In the course of preparing the broadcasts I have been privileged to discuss many matters alluded to above, and much else of great interest, with three distinguished scientists. Dr Miriam Rothschild FRS is renowned as a natural historian, her interests irradiating widely from her central scholarship in the field of entomology, particularly the study of fleas. Dr Donald Griffin, of Rockefeller and now Harvard University, likewise is acknowledged as a world leader in his field of study of consciousness in animals. Sir John Eccles FRS Australia's only living Nobel laureate in Physiology or Medicine, has spent a lifetime in physiological analysis of neural function and during the past two to three decades has written a number of books on the body–mind problem, which is an all-consuming interest for him.

Large segments of the transcripts of these discussions have been included in the chapters. In asking questions aimed at eliciting their views it has been necessary in a few instances to pose as questions matters I have discussed already in the text, but this small amount of reiteration is essential so that the reader knows precisely what they have been asked to speak about. Because they are verbatim transcripts, a change of style and tempo results, and this, hopefully, diversifies the presentation. The remainder of the transcripts of these three discussions, which cover issues additional to those incorporated in the chapters, are reproduced in the Appendix.

In an endeavour to share the excitement inherent in the cornucopia of fascinating questions concerning brain function in man and animals, I will traverse matters as diverse as, for example, the evocation of long-lost memories by electrical stimulation of the brain surface, the fashion in which the midbrain orchestrates arousal or alternatively sleep and dreams, the remarkable learning abilities of dolphins, questions of despair and sensing of death in animals, the linguistic capacities of apes, and the issue of any nascent awareness in creatures as low in the scale of life as invertebrates. To place contemporary thinking in perspective, some historical ideas on mind and brain function in Egyptian, Greek, Oriental and mediaeval European cultures will be briefly and selectively recounted in chapter 2. Except perhaps for the segment of the discussion with Sir John Eccles on Descartes at the end of chapter 2 (which is directly pertinent to the main theme of the book), the reader may prefer to go from chapter 1 straight on to chapter 3, which deals with consciousness in the animals.

The notion is advanced that a powerful force favouring the emergence of dim awareness and consciousness may have been the imperative to coalesce the inflow from different senses—touch, sight, smell and hearing—to form a coherent picture of the outside world, a cross-matching procedure.

*The Pinnacle of Life* presents a panorama of the increasing complexity of animal behaviour with ascent of the evolutionary tree, and has a central theme that a creature may be said to have a mind if it is shown to have intentions bespeaking the formation of images or a model of the world. This theme is followed from the knowledge of bees, beavers, dogs and the great apes, to the emergence of man, a creature which can fashion an object for an imagined eventuality—the anthropological definition of man and also Aristotle's definition of the artist. In its latter parts, the book examines the way the natural world, and the delight in it, has engraved a particular character to consciousness, as is manifest by the emergence of artistic expression.

# 1

# The ultimate challenge

The ultimate challenge to human ingenuity is the unravelling of the nature of consciousness—the awareness of being alive. It is a major preoccupation of the inquiring human spirit. It is the scientific challenge with the greatest implication for the human future. Einstein and Freud in their renowned correspondence identified it as the most pressing task for humanity. Einstein remarked: 'As for me, the normal objective of my thought affords no insight into the dark places of human will and feeling...Man has within him a lust for hatred and destruction.'

Understanding the mainsprings of aggression, hate and violence, and the counterparts of altruism, benevolence and generosity of spirit, will be crucial to charting the future. The challenge is not an esoteric or academic issue. As Winston Churchill said in his acceptance of the Nobel Prize in 1953,

> Since Alfred Nobel died in 1896 we have entered an age of storm and tragedy. The power of man has grown in every sphere except over himself... We in Europe and the Western world who have planned for health and social security, who have

marvelled at the triumphs of medicine and science, and who have aimed at justice and freedom for all, have nevertheless been witness to famine, misery, cruelty and destruction before which pale the deeds of Attila and Gengis Khan ... We have lived to see a world marred by cleavages and threatened by discords even graver and more violent than those which convulsed Europe after the fall of the Roman Empire.

In endeavouring to analyse and discuss the centrepoint of existence of every human being—the sense of self—the approach I shall follow will be Darwinian and thus that of evolutionary biology. However, the examination of the issues has been anything but the prerogative of medical biologists. Questions of consciousness and mind have preoccupied philosophers, writers, poets and natural scientists for millennia. Virginia Woolf in her essay on Montaigne in the *Common Reader* wrote:

Once, at Bar-Le-Duc, Montaigne saw a portrait Rene, King of Italy, had painted of himself, and asked, 'Why is it not, in like manner, lawful for everyone to draw himself with a pen, as he did with a crayon?'

Offhand one might reply, not only is it lawful but nothing could be easier. Other people may evade us but our own features are almost too familiar. Let us begin. And then, when we attempt the task, the pen falls from our fingers; it is a matter of profound, mysterious, and overwhelming difficulty.

The phantom is through the mind and out the window before we can lay salt on its tail, or slowly sinking and returning to the profound darkness which it has lit up momentarily with a wandering light.

Montaigne himself says:

'Tis a rugged road, more so than it seems, to
follow a pace so rambling and uncertain as that of
the soul; to penetrate the dark profundities of its
intricate internal windings, to choose and lay hold
of so many nimble notions, 'tis a new and
extraordinary undertaking, and that withdraws us
from the common and most recommended
employments of the world.

Now I can say our discussions will take us down
diverse pathways. In the first stages I shall deal with
several facets of thought about consciousness and
mind down the ages, and also discuss some pivotal
facts emerging from studies by brain surgeons, neurologists and neuroscientists. Following the historical
account, we will talk about the issue of consciousness
in animals, particularly bearing upon communicative
capacity, and also the issue of self-awareness in the
great apes, as revealed by experiments with a mirror.
Some interesting studies of animals throw light on
puzzling phenomena in humans such as voodoo, death
from bone-pointing in Aborigines, and the matter of
psychogenic sudden death.

Following this we will traverse some of the frontiers
of knowledge apparent from clinical medical studies
of the brain. In particular, I will deal with the evocation of memory by electrical stimulation of the brain
surface in conscious humans during brain surgery
under local anaesthesia, and the remarkable insights
on organisation of brain function revealed by studies
of patients in whom it was necessary to surgically cut
the 200 million fibres joining the two hemispheres of
the brain (the so-called split-brain humans). I will also
recount some ideas about the brain operating in modules, as perhaps shown in the instance of a person who
knows many languages but who has had a stroke. The
person may have lost one or more languages, but one

has been retained; and it may not be the language most recently learned or pertinent to the society in which they live. Also, we will deal with the observations coincident to neurosurgical therapy where electrical stimulation of deep centres in the brain succeeds in invoking orgasmic states and various pleasures.

Thereupon I will present the other face to awareness: sleep.

> Oh mistress, mistress night
> thou giver of sleep to mortals and all their toils
> Come forth from the cosmic dark, come, come on
> thy wings.

This, from Orestes of Euripides, brings us also to dreaming in humans and animals and the significance of dreams.

Then I will recount some of the most exciting ideas concerning the evolution of the brain and the emergence of human society, mythology and art. In trying to meld several elements, I will bias the focus to some extent on one particular facet of the artistic, creative process that has impressed many people deeply—that is, the recurrent and overwhelming influence of the pantheistic within consciousness, the sense in man of a oneness with nature and the universe, which pervades the being, and has been the genesis of some of the greatest writing and poetry. For many human beings there is an overt delight in the feeling of being a part of the physical world, involving, as it does, the awe of the cosmos and the physical pleasure of the forests, rivers and oceans. To quote Byron from *Childe Harold's Pilgrimage*,

> There is a pleasure in the pathless woods,
> There is a rapture in the lonely shore,
> There is a society, where none intrudes,
> By the deep sea, and music in its roar:

I love not man the less, but Nature more,
From these our interviews in which I steal
From all I may be or have been before,
To mingle with the Universe, and feel
What I can ne'er express, yet cannot all conceal.

The question of whether there is any aesthetic sense in animals, as, for example, in birdsongs or bowerbird display, also arises.

In the final chapter of the book, I will lead from the subject of conscious delight in the natural world to recent data on brain function and some of the diametrically opposed ideas on the nature of consciousness.

Of a story, the late Samuel Goldwyn remarked it should begin with an earthquake and work up to a climax. We will probably not see this here, but I hope we will cover a lot of ground that should be of great interest to the curious. At the outset I should remark also that on this canvas we will inevitably, in an historical context if no other way, encounter many religious ideas on the matter of body and mind, or the soul, and the great divide between mind and body that has been made by theologians and many philosophers. Michael Gazzaniga in his book *The Social Brain* recalls how, when his mentor, Nobel laureate Roger Sperry, returned from a symposium on consciousness held at the Vatican, he recounted that the Pope had addressed the gathering of scientists. The Pope had said, in essence, that the scientists could have the brain and the Church would have the mind. Gazzaniga remarks, with humour, that this was not perhaps exactly what his Holiness Pope Paul VI had said at that time. Actually the transcript reads:

To be sure when you speak of 'conciousness' you do not refer to the moral conscience: the very

5

rigour of your methods ensure that you do not leave that strictly scientific domain which belongs to you.

And he adds:

But who does not see the close connection between the cerebral mechanisms, as they appear from the results of experimentation, and the higher processes which concern the strictly spiritual activity of the soul? Your labours are valued by us, as you see, because of the domain in which they are pursued, because of their close affinities with that which is of supreme interest to a spiritual power such as Ours—the domain of the moral and religious activities of man.

## THE SURVIVAL ADVANTAGE OF CONSCIOUSNESS

I will espouse a Darwinian view. That is, the phenomenon of conciousness has arisen progressively in the course of evolution of animal life because its emergence, elaboration and refinement has conferred great survival advantage on the species. The advantage lies in a creature being able to exercise options. By images in the mind—be they the most rudimentary or the most elaborate—the animal may examine the possible outcome of its actions. It can choose a course and in so doing may meld its instinctive memory, the legacy of the past in the particular species, with such experience as it has already had in the course of its own life.

Henry James, the distinguished American writer, expressed the view concerning exercise of options as 'mind being a theatre of simultaneous possibilities— the selection of some and suppression of the rest', whereas William James, eminent psychologist and philosopher (and brother of Henry), suggested 'consciousness is what you might expect in a nervous system grown too large to steer itself'. The point is that judging a course of action is likely to be much more successful than simple reflex response to a situation which, in fact, may cause the creature to be killed. Some evaluation or weighing between instinctive urges and desires and the results of its own experience to date may be more successful; thus the animal survives, to hand on to its progeny the genes that help to contrive this ability.

John Crook of the UK, who has written extensively on this subject, interprets it as a processing of the information provided by the senses to form an analogue of the exterior. This results in the external world being 'seen', reflecting the ascendancy of vision in human life. Comparison of the input with the existing 'map' may alert the animal or human to novelty, and thus cause focusing of attention, with other matters receding to the periphery of the stream of consciousness.

## SELF-AWARENESS

The zenith of the process with emergence of conciousness is, of course, what Hughlings Jackson, the great English neurologist, termed the inward turning of consciousness, or self-awareness. This is the inner eye scrutinising the actual mode of thinking itself. The process may lay bare the mainsprings of motivation. It makes the mind transparent to itself. Isaiah Berlin, of Oxford University, put it that the mind becomes the subject and object of itself. Now this ability to build scenarios, the placing of yourself as the central actor, allows the building of images in a situation, and these may present several options. The capacity to deliberately balance two alternatives and weigh them is probably the reason we are persuaded of 'free will'. Though the elements we weigh may be predetermined in certain fashions, this machinery and the sense it gives of decision is of high survival value, allowing, as it does, the anticipation of the next steps and appropriate planning.

Nicholas Humphrey of Cambridge University, who studied gorilla behaviour, sees the emergence of self-awareness during evolution as dictated—indeed generated—by social pressures. To hold a society together, there is great advantage in understanding one's fellows. Insight into one's own mental processes allows prediction and sometimes control of what others desire or will do.*

In taking an evolutionary view, it seems to me to follow incontrovertibly that consciousness is indivisibly a function of the brain. In relation to the so-called body–mind problem, without the function of the brain there is no mind, no consciousness, or, for that matter, no soul if one wishes to term the pervading sense of self in that fashion. As J.Z. Young, the distinguished anatomist, says in his book *Philosophy and the Brain*,

The evidence shows that I and my brain are one;

---

\* There are, however, contrary views on this. Friedrich Nietzsche in *The Gay Science* says: 'Consciousness is the last and latest development of the organic, and hence also what is most unfinished and unstrong. Consciousness gives rise to countless errors that lead an animal or man to perish sooner than necessary—"exceeding destiny", as Homer puts it. If the conserving association of the instincts were not so very much more powerful ... humanity would have to perish of its misjudgements and its fantasies ... in short its consciousness.' Nietzsche also remarked in *Zarathustra*: 'One must have chaos ... to give birth to a dancing star', which could be an adventurous administrative principle for a ballet company.

without a brain I should be nothing. If the person is inseparable from his brain it is senseless to ask which of them controls the other.

He adds:

Descartes' statement 'I think, therefore I am' is better replaced by 'I know that I am alive'. Which emphasises that knowledge is a property of the operation of the physical body and this mitigates the problems of dualism.
The fact of human consciousness seems to separate us from the rest of the living world, and yet there is abundant evidence that all mental events are correlated with brain processes.

Bertrand Russell also remarks that the formula 'I think, therefore I am' is itself not very sound. There is a concealed notion that thinking is a self-conscious process. Otherwise one might as well say 'I walk, therefore I am.'

## THE DEVELOPMENT OF CONSCIOUSNESS

Earlier this century, Julian Huxley, H.G. Wells and G.P. Wells, in their great book *The Science of Life*, reflected that: 'We have seen every reason to suppose that life is evolved from not life. Living matter from matter that had never been alive.'

In their view, if we are not to break the principle of continuity, which is at the root of any connected thinking about the world and is revealed clearly in the material side of development and evolution, we must suppose that consciousness such as we possess has evolved just as muscles, nerves and eyes have—that is, out of undifferentiated protoplasm and its less-specialised activities. The authors draw an analogy in describing fishes that give violent electric shocks. At first glance there seems to be no bridge between this power and the capacities of other animals, although as delicate instrumentation was developed in scientific laboratories it became clear that virtually all life processes were accompanied by at least some minute electrical activity. But in the eel, special 'machinery' has been built up which intensifies the electrical happenings. Huxley and his co-authors proposed that perhaps this sort of thing could happen with the mind with a transition from dim awareness, a dim striving at lower levels, through to consciousness in higher animals and humans. Evolution confirms our intuition to ascribe to animals such as dogs and mice a consciousness, although we can have little idea what, if any, dim awareness and perception exists in frogs and reptiles, for example.

Concerning the mind of the human being, the three authors quote Lotka:

'To say the necessary condition for writing these words is the willing of the author to write them, and to say a necessary condition for writing of them is a certain state and configuration of the material of his brain, these two statements are probably merely two ways of saying the same thing.

That is, a human is the portion of the stuff of reality organised so that it is intensely conscious—not mind *and* body, but body and mind in one. Bertrand Russell suggested succinctly that the difference between matter and mind is merely one of arrangement. This concept of how the organism experiences brain happenings, the concept of one mind and body, has since the time of Spinoza been called monism, and is the flat opposite of the extreme dualism of Descartes.

Roger Sperry says:

Can conscious experience exist apart from the brain? Dualism, affirming existence of independent mental and physical worlds says 'yes' and opens the door to a conscious afterlife, and to many kinds of supernatural, paranormal, and other worldly beliefs. Monism, on the other hand, restricts its answers to one-world dimensions and says 'no' to an independent existence of conscious mind apart from the functioning brain.

This matter we will deal with further on. But, as is well known, Descartes in the seventeenth century held that animals were automata while only a human being had a conscious soul. He proposed it to be the greatest of all prejudices, retained from our infancy, that beasts could think. He thought the soul communicated with the body through the pineal gland (a pea-like structure on the upper surface of the brain).

Before we go further with this matter of consciousness as the most exciting and powerful of all emergents in the evolution of living creatures, and before we trace some historical thinking which leads up to contemporary ideas, it is best that I cover some aspects of present knowledge of brain organisation and function.

## BRAIN ARCHITECTURE AND CONSCIOUSNESS

There are some facts on architecture or spatial organisation derived from studies done by brain surgeons, clinical neurologists and experimental neuroscientists. As Wilder Penfield, the great Canadian neurosurgeon, points out, consciousness continues regardless of what area of cerebral cortex (the folded grey matter on the surface of the brain) is removed.

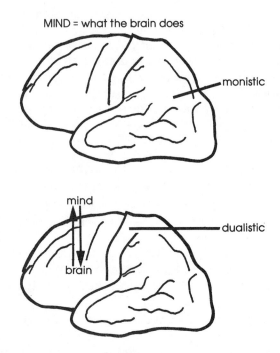

The two views of mind–brain relationship.

However, consciousness is inevitably lost when the function of the diencephalon (the higher brain stem) is interrupted by injury, pressure, disease or local epileptic discharge. All regions of the brain may be involved in normal conscious processes, but the indispensable substratum of consciousness lies outside the cerebral cortex, probably in the upper brain stem.

Apart from physiological experiment, this recognition of the role of the brain stem came from an experiment of nature—the influenza epidemic of 1918, when a particularly virulent form of the virus entered the brain and devoured neurones. The neurological

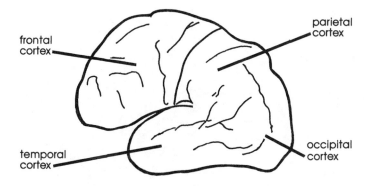

A diagram of the left hemisphere of the brain showing the four main lobes.

catastrophe that followed brain infection was called encephalitis lethargica, because the afflicted subjects were unable to maintain alert, waking states. Such sleeping sickness was often irreversible. The discovery by Constantine von Economo that killed cells were localised in the brain stem was, as Allan Hobson, professor of psychiatry at Harvard University, points out, a turning point in the history of the attempt to understand the brain basis of conciousness. Von Economo saw that cells supporting the sleep/wakefulness state may be localised in the brain stem and that the alert/wake state might be supported by these cells. He did not appreciate that the localisation of damage also indicated a chemical targeting by the virus, and that the cells killed by the virus were in a region of the brain called the substantia nigra, which is blackish because of a pigment in the cells. These black-pigmented cells are also involved in motor control. Another aftermath of the flu epidemic, because of

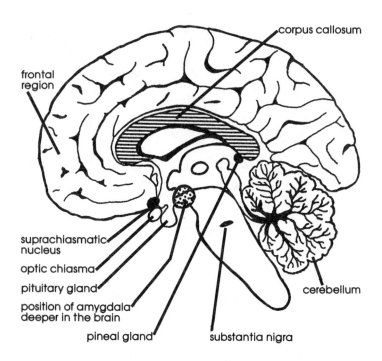

The brain divided from front to back in the middle (sagittal section). The position of the substantia nigra in the midbrain (involved in Parkinson's disease) is shown, also the pineal gland (Descartes' seat of the soul), the suprachiasmatic nucleus, which orchestrates daily rhythms (see chapter 5), and the corpus callosum, which conducts signals between the two sides of the brain.

damage to this substantia nigra, was Parkinsonism, or Parkinson's disease.

The actual system in the brain stem was called the reticular activating system, or RAS for short. The neurones (nerve cells) of the reticular system, which are located at many places in the brain stem in groups of thousands, are structurally unusual. Their message-

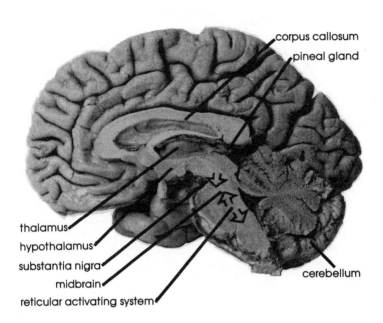

corpus callosum
pineal gland
thalamus
hypothalamus
substantia nigra
midbrain
reticular activating system
cerebellum

A photograph of a human brain which has been divided
by a cut in the middle from front to back (sagittal section).
Those structures referred to in the text are indicated.

carrying processes may divide in two, and one branch
descends down the brain stem while the other goes
upwards to the cortex. Processes from the pool of
neurones can fan out over the entire cortex. Thus the
cells can influence a very great part of the brain.

Indeed, a single electrical pulse of one-thousandth
of a second's duration in a particular part of the reticular system will set up a burst of rhythmic activity in
widespread areas of the cerebral cortex on both sides
of the brain. Areas at the top of the RAS are organised
for action upon local areas further up in grey matter
of the cortex, so assisting the process of focus of
attention.

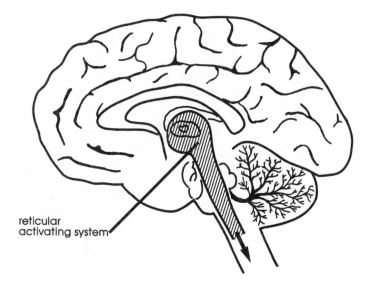

reticular
activating system

A diagrammatic representation of the region of the
reticular activating system involved in arousal and in sleep.
Nerve cells in this system send large numbers of projections
up to the grey mantle or cortex of the brain, and
corresponding pathways descend from the cortex to
nuclear aggregations of the reticular activating system.

Wilder Penfield emphasised that the RAS acts as a
unifier or organiser, in that it coordinates the cortex
and lower brain stem control centres into a functional
unity of up-and-down traffic. Neuronal activity within
the reticular activating system is the indispensible
substratum of consciousness. But Penfield says to call
it a 'centrecephalon' or to say it is a block of brain
where consciousness is located would be to call back
Descartes and offer him a substitute for the pineal
gland as the seat of the soul.

However, much of the choreography of consciousness does reside in the brain stem, and Jean-Pierre Changeaux of the Collège de France likens it to the console of an organ in the orchestration of consciousness. Furthermore, as we will discuss later, surgical division of the corpus callosum (the 200–300 million fibres of the great commissure or transmission lines joining the two hemispheres of the brain in humans) can result in two independent states of consciousness—the one on the left side having no idea of what the right side of the brain knows and can act upon. This crucial finding indicates that rather than any unitary awareness being resident in the brain stem, it is rather an essential orchestrating ingredient to the conscious process going on in either hemisphere under these circumstances.

In amphibians and reptiles the reticular midbrain areas are the areas that predominate since a primitive cortex is only just beginning to emerge. This rudimentary cortex is represented by the optic lobes in reptiles. It is perhaps conceivable that some of the neural machinery to subserve early dim perception and awareness is present in lower animals at this brain stem level. Many of our concepts of the role of the reticular system have come from studies of lower animals, but Fred Plum, professor of neurology at Cornell Medical School, New York Hospital, drawing on a vast knowledge of neurological diseases, also concludes that cognitive consciousness in humans depends on ascending inputs that originate far below the geographic borders of the brain cortex. Nonetheless, Plum states that, in humans, severe bilateral (but not unilateral) impairment of the cerebral cortical mantle can result in coma—which emphasises the difference between humans and animals.

## THE INFLUENCE OF THE MIND ON BODY PROCESSES AND VICE VERSA

At this stage in the book we should perhaps consider one of the greatest mysteries in analysis: the way in which integrated neural activity, or brain function involved with thought, can itself modify neural function. The nature or intent of the thought process can direct the searchlight of the subject's attention so as to recruit other cerebral functions that were previously quiescent. The situation is not (as is often the case) that some sensory inflow from the external world will focus attention on particular events, but rather that the act of thinking about an issue will, of itself, initiate action in nerve cell populations at a distance. Neurophysiological studies have found that the focusing of attention will modify the activity of particular cerebral cells. Recordings from specific cells in conscious cats reveal that these cells may fire in quite different fashion, according to whether the cat's attention is deliberately directed to a particular object, such as a mouse, or whether no such process is in train.

A good example of the irradiating and determinant effect of thinking on neural processes would be any thought that initiates cascades of reaction in visceral processes. For example, a person entering a restaurant and reading the menu may conjure up a picture of some of the dishes and be aware of the fact that he or she is salivating. Another excellent example would be the relaxed state with the mind wandering and settling on a sexual fantasy. It is not a linguistic or language phenomenon. It can be played out entirely in mental pictures. Indeed, progress of the situation in so-called real time in the mind may eventually result in obvious reactions in the viscera, whether the person is male or female. This issue of thinking in pictures and the widespread bodily effects is of considerable importance. Some of the arguments about consciousness have suggested that it is a peculiarly human phenomenon and that the main determinant of the emergence of this capacity in humans resides in language. But although language is a pre-eminent element of consciousness and thinking, it seems that fantasies with images not involving any linguistic function can clearly have widespread visceral effects—or, for that matter, may be part of many strategies. As every doctor knows, the mind can have profound effects on bodily visceral processes, to the extent of being able to set in train major organic disease.

And, of course, in the same vein of interaction, the function of the mind is easy prey to chemical changes in the body. This ranges from the very nature of the vital regulatory processes, such as thirst, to the way in which intoxication with alcohol or drugs such as opium can distort the brain and thus the mind function. As Herodotus said in the fifth century BC, 'When the body is seriously deranged it is not surprising that the mind is also.'

To expand a little on this issue of chemistry affecting the mind: thirst is a classic example, although I could use the hunger for salt in a similar fashion. With thirst we have a whole piece of brain machinery ready and poised to take over the stream of consciousness and to arouse the subject with a specific desire to drink fluid. Attention may be directed exclusively to this end. Accordingly, the subject searches and drinks their fill to satisfaction, and thereupon the sensation disappears. How come?

It appears that the controlling cells are in the middle of the brain. These sensor cells are specially wired up so that if there's an increase in the salt concentration of the blood bathing them (being, for all practical purposes, the salt concentration of all the blood in the body), the cells will shrink, and this shrinking causes them to fire electrical impulses like a machine gun along pathways that have now been well mapped. The result is that somehow the stream of consciousness is commandeered by the sense of thirst. What the sense of thirst actually is, is still a great mystery. Certainly one component feeding into the brain from the periphery localises this sensation to the mouth—the so called dry-mouth sensation. This can be explained by the fact that the chemical conditions of the blood that fired up our sensors of salt concentration in the brain have also, by another mechanism, slowed down and stopped salivary secretion. So the mouth is indeed dry, and this sensation is conveyed to the brain.

But this is only a back-up. Experiments in which a thirsty animal is allowed to drink water, but arranged so the water doesn't enter the stomach and get absorbed, reveal that the sensation of thirst remains. Similarly, if you were to remove the stomach of a human or an animal, the hunger sensation would remain during food deprivation, even though you would have eliminated the possibility of stomach contractions and the so-called hunger pains.

So we see a central control system ready to take over the mind and direct it in specific directions if the chemistry of the blood changes. This is vital to the wellbeing of the organism and of high survival value. If the situation gets worse, as it might for a shipwrecked sailor, the sensation can mount to a diabolical craving. Thirst totally rivets the attention of the subject.

But to emphasise how beautifully the machinery of nature works, it should be noted that the loss of water from the body—from the skin, the lungs and by urine formation—is continuous. If, as loss continued, every tiny deviation of the salt concentration of blood were to activate the thirst mechanism, it would be all we could think about. There would be little chance of sustained concentration by the poet on couplets, the ballerina on her 64 fouettes, or the businessman on the interest rates. So nature has arranged that there is a threshold, literally a step over which the change must pass. That is, the change in concentration must be big enough before our character thirst is allowed an entrance, and can occupy centre stage of the mind and have most or all attention directed to it and by it. Obviously the same thing is true of all other vegetative high-survival-value functions which are genetically programmed and extensively pre-wired in our brain— for example, the drives of hunger, sexual desire and maternal behaviour, the acts of territorial defence, and the appetite for specific minerals such as salt. When the appropriate change of body chemistry or hormone concentration occurs, specific sensors or receptors alert and fire up neural groups dedicated to this particular behaviour in these deeper parts of the brain, and the attention and stream of consciousness is directed to the relevant issues that will lead eventually to gratification of the perceived need.

So this is one major facet of the way in which bodily processes can direct the flow of the mind. Mysterious though it may be, the chemistry of the brain dictates the scenario of conciousness, its stream in real time.

# 2

# Some early ideas on the brain and mind

The history of ideas on consciousness and mind is long and diverse. The matter has puzzled humanity for millennia. In the Bible, chapters of Kings, Isaiah, and Jeremiah, dating back 5000 years, identify the heart as the source of motor behaviour, and the kidneys with the capacity for emotions.

The Egyptians were said to believe that the heart was the centre of consciousness, although an Egyptian military surgeon about 5000 years ago noted that after a person suffered concussion the leg and foot were paralysed and the upper extremity became spastic. Reporting his 48 cases of head and neck injury, he noted: 'If you examinest a man with a smash in the temple, if thou callest to him he cannot speak.' In case 31 he tells us that after dislocating vertebrae in the neck, 'The patient was not conscious of his arms and legs, but his phallus was erect and he urinated and ejaculated unconsciously.' As Jean-Pierre Changeaux remarks in his book *Neuronal Man*, the cases provide a precise description of symptoms now known to be involved with brain and skull injury, and the account is given with a simple objectivity and without magical formulae. The military surgeon even noted some ailments that ought not to be treated—a humane perception of the doctor's role.

This clear evidence of the role of the brain and spinal column was not very influential, however. For centuries afterwards, the heart was espoused as the source of life. It is indeed there, writes Lucretius, 'that fear and terror leap, it is there that joy gently throbs'.

With the Greeks it is possible to see two paths of thinking. Before the fifth century BC they appear to have regarded the heart as the thinking, movement-controlling organ, and this certainly persisted with Aristotle (384–322 BC).

In *De Juventute*, Aristotle enquires where in the body the seat of life is to be found. He observes that the central principle of nutrition, which is to control the nourishment of the whole body, must be centrally situated; and says definitely that the heart is the central organ both in sensation and in nutrition. Aristotle regarded the heart as the seat of life in all its aspects and was influenced among other things by observing that in the developing chick embryo the heart was first apparent. He observed also that the brain was not sensitive when mechanically touched. In several places he says it is in the heart that the soul is set aglow.

As speech comes from the thorax, and thought precedes speech, it seemed to follow that the organ of thought was in the thorax, and probably was the heart.

As a matter of fact, literature is full of the idea. For example, 'Let the words of my mouth, and the meditation of my heart, be alway acceptable in thy sight, O Lord.' And of course, in Shakespeare's *Merchant of Venice*: 'Tell me, where is fancy bred, or in the heart or in the head?' Myfanwy Piper, the librettist of Benjamin Britten's *Death in Venice*, has Aschenbach sing of his 'beating mind', just as Prospero in *The Tempest* would walk a turn or two 'to still my beating mind'.

It is amusing to speculate what Aristotle would have made of heart transplants. But, as Geoffrey Lloyd of Darwin College, Cambridge, concludes, Aristotle's misconception about the brain does not detract from his emphasis on the study of nature by observation. The highest faculty that humans possess is reason (*nous*), and the supreme activity is contemplation. Hence, observation of the external parts of animals is not enough, and it must be supplemented by the use of dissection. The aim of natural science is to reveal the cause of phenomena. Incidentally, Charles Darwin regarded Aristotle as the greatest of the ancient biologists.

Aristotle applied the same analysis of causation to both natural objects and artefacts (manmade objects), but he recognised certain differences in the way in which it applies in the two fields. The most important difference concerns the final cause, for whereas in artificial production this is supplied by conscious deliberation of the craftsman or artist, Artistotle denies that any conscious purposes are at work in nature. He postulates that there is no divine mind controlling natural changes from the outside.

Clearly, the landmark character of Aristotle's view lies in the notion of the living creature as a complex whole. Soul is no separate entity that inhabits the body during the lifetime of the animal. It is indeed the actuality of the body—that which makes the living creature what it is. Further, Geoffrey Lloyd remarks:

> While Plato stands as the first major exponent of the dualist view, and what has become to be called the mind/body problem, Aristotle may legitimately be considered the first major exponent of the opposite monistic view, according to which mind

and body are considered not as different substances, but rather as different aspects of a single complex entity.

Herophilus and Erasistratus represent the highwater mark in Alexandrian biology. They worked in Alexandria in the first half of the third century BC and had the support of the Ptolemys. They were admired by the great Galen, who lived in the second century AD. They were the first to practise dissection of the human body, which neither the Hippocratic writers nor Aristotle did. Several writers mention vivisection on humans as well as dissection of the dead. They cut open living men, criminals obtained out of the prison from the king. It is good to report that one man, Celsus, took exception—'To cut open the bodies of living men is both cruel and superfluous'—but the group of doctors involved, called the Dogmatists, defended themselves against the charge of inhumanity by claiming that the good outweighed the evil, that it was not cruel to seek remedies for multitudes of innocent people of future ages by means of the sacrifice of a small number of criminals. Considering that the ancients regularly tortured slaves, and that new poisons where tried out on criminals, it seems feasible that the Ptolemys allowed vivisection on criminals.

Herophilus worked on the brain and recognised it as the centre of the nervous system. He recognised the ventricles (the fluid-filled cavities) of the brain and identified in them the choroid plexus (a plexus of veins and arteries held together by delicate membranes, named 'choroid' because of resemblance to the outer membrane of the foetus, the 'chorion'). He and Erasistratus distinguished between motor and sensory nerves and distinguished these from ligaments and tendons. Herophilus established that the pulse derived from the heart and undertook a systematic classification of differences from normal in relation to character and rate, which is interesting because Herophilus had no accurate means of timing the pulse.

Erasistratus was a cautious doctor, criticising remedies such as blood-letting and purging which, as we know, were inclined to part body and soul. He actually inserted a tube into an artery to investigate the pulse.

With Galen in the second century AD there was a great advance in knowledge, although he drew on the findings of the Alexandrian physicians four centuries earlier. Galen investigated the nervous system by systematic division of the spinal cord on one side or right across to determine the loss of function, paralysis, at different levels. Observing surgery by physicians, he saw the devastating effect on speech caused by cutting of the recurrent laryngeal nerve (which travels to the vocal cords); he also showed the effect on vocalisation in animals when the nerve was cut, for the pig ceased to squeal.

Sir David Ross remarks that it is a disappointing feature of Aristotle's physiology that he did not recognise the importance of the brain, believing that the cold slimy spongelike structure overlying the respiratory passages served to cool the blood. He did note that humans had a larger brain than any other animal but did not draw the conclusion that this is what distinguishes our species. Indeed, he rejected the idea.

Probably the discoverer of the function of the brain in sensation in Hellenic thought was Alcmaeon (c. 500 BC), who has been described as the founder of empirical or observational psychology. He practised dissection and discovered passages (pathways), lesions of which prevented communication of sensation. Others, Diogenes, Democritus and Plato, had argued in favour of the brain. Democritus wrote: 'The brain, guardian of thoughts or intelligence', and added, 'It contains bonds of the soul.'

Aristotle's misconception is surprising in light of the fact that those who generated the Hippocratic writings (460–377 BC) had stated the clear deduction based on clinical data. For example, the Hippocratic writings caution against widely probing an open wound in the temple skull because it could provoke movements on the opposite side of the body. Other writings challenge the practice of assigning a divine source for the cause of epilepsy: 'The cause of epilepsy lies in the brain, for the brain is the organ of all psychic processes both normal and abnormal. If the brain is irritated, intelligence is impaired, the brain enters into spasms, and the whole body convulses.'

And further, what Fred Plum suggests to be perhaps the best-known writing in Greek medicine: 'Eyes, ears, tongues, hands and feet act in accordance with the discernment of the brain. Pleasure, joy, laughter and jests, as well as sorrows, pain, grief and tears originate in the brain.' As Plum says, it would be difficult to say it better today.

In threading our way through some paths of Greek learning and thought about the nature of humans and consciousness we have centred on the rational analysis. It is important to note the irrational element in Greek thought in relation to explanation of behaviour. Professor E.R. Dodds of Oxford University extensively analysed this in his book *The Greeks and the Irrational.*

'*Ate*' is a state of mind, a temporary clouding or bewildering of the normal consciousness. It is a partial and temporary insanity and is ascribed not to physiological and psychological causes but to an external 'demonic' agency. Dodds regards it as much more than a fashion of speaking. Thus, Agamemnon in *The Iliad* says:

> Not I, not I was the cause of this act, Zeus and my portion and the Erinys who walks in darkness: they it was who in the assembly put wild *Ate* in my understanding on the day when I arbitrarily took Achilles' prize from him.

Dodds remarks:

> One of the things which strikes us is the deepened awareness of human insecurity and human helplessness which has its religious correlate in the feeling of divine hostility—not in the sense that Diety is thought of as evil, but in the sense that an over-mastering Power and Wisdom for ever holds man down, keeps him from rising above his station.

As in *Antigone*:

> Ageless the Master holds for ever the shimmering courts of Olympus,
> For time approaching and time hereafter and time forgotten, one rule stands:
> That greatness never should touch the life of man without destruction.

Dodds adds:

> Homeric man does not possess the concept of will (which developed curiously late in Greece), and therefore cannot possess the concept of 'free will'. To ask whether Homer's people are determinists or libertarians is a fantastic anachronism: the question has never occurred to them, they wouldn't know what you are talking about.

Joseph Needham in his epic work on science and civilisation in China (I understand that volumes on medicine are to join the some fifteen preceding ones within the next couple of years) writes of the Sung dynasty (960–1279 AD), the greatest flowering of indigenous Chinese science, and its Neo-Confucianism, when they had a view of the world congruent with that of the natural sciences. Needham quotes Chu Hsi, the twelfth-century commentator on Confucianism: 'Animals were not seen as conscious having a material constitution opaque and gross through which the full possibilities of nature cannot manifest themselves, just as the light of the sun or the moon is partially obscured by the walls of a mat shed.' Confucianism sees the inequality of endowment and badness in human beings, and also in their capacities—as Needham says, 'in some ways foreshadowing modern genetics'.

In relation to any concept of soul, Chu Hsi was quite clear that 'individual human spirits do not survive'.

Someone asked whether at the time of death a man's consciousness is dissipated and scattered. Chu Hsi answered that

> it was not merely dissipated but completely finished. The *Chii* (the breath of life of the body) comes to an end and so does consciousness. The opinion of the Buddhists that human spirits may survive as ghosts, and be reincarnated in later human beings is absolutely wrong. That which dies disappears and does not return. Of changeless in the Universe, there is nothing but *Li* (the universal principle of organisation of organic matter). No creatures are eternal, all are subject to change and mortality.

In the analysis of Indian ideas of the mind, it is said by Steven Collins of the University of Bristol that in no case can we assume anything simply comparable to Western mind–body dualism, nor has much attention been paid to the specific body–mind problem. Any physical location of consciousness has been rather a mystical physiology; circles or centres of energy with different kinds of consciousness are associated with different centres.

The religious context of Indian thought influences ideas of mind with overriding moral and spiritual attitudes. Generally speaking, the senses and mind are regarded as appetitive, as desiring, grasping and relishing their objects in a very active sensing or marrying them. In the unenlightened this rapaciousness is wayward and uncontrollable. Enlightenment requires control to let it proceed and let it be seen as it really is.

The *Katha Upanishad* (sixth–fifth century BC) uses a familiar image:

> Know the self as the chariot owner (that is he who is carried inactively by it), and the body as the chariot. Know awareness as the driver, the mind as the reins. The senses, they say, are the horses, sense objects the path they range over. The self, joined to mind and senses, wise men say is the experiencer. He who is without understanding, his mind is ever unharnessed, his senses are out of control, as bad horses are for the charioteer.

A similar theme is in the *Bhagavad Gita* (third century BC): 'When a man's mind follows after the wandering senses, his wisdom is carried away, as the wind [carries away] a ship on water.'

In the Vijnanavada school of Buddhism, objects of thought and perception are said to arise from within the mind:

> Just as on the ocean, waves stirred up by the wind dance and roll unceasingly, so the mind sea, constantly stirred up by sense objects, dances and

> rolls with its multiform consciousness—waves.
> (*Lankavatara Sutra*)

It should be emphasised that this cameo from the enormous corpus of Oriental literature does not begin to encompass the diverse viewpoints. The distinguished poet Harold Stewart of Kyoto points out that there is extensive material in Chinese and Buddhist writings reflecting a different conclusion to that quoted by Professor Needham. Indian literature includes contemplation of exalted states experienced by those practising yoga for deepening and expanding consciousness. Fritjof Kapra, the physicist and philosopher, emphasises that the rich tradition of Indian philosophy has generated a spectrum of schools from extreme materialism to extreme idealism, from absolute monism, through dualism to complete pluralism.

Returning to our odyssey of European thought, we see how St Augustine (AD 354–436) made brilliant observations on memory, noted by Dr Plum:

> That of the senses involves experience that is
> built from perceptions—tactile, olfactory, visual,
> the strength of an impression (i.e. attention) is
> critical to the persistence of a memory, and
> repetition and arrangement may aid this function.

Yet there was no interest in how the brain may work as a biological entity to achieve this. It was the soul that encompassed the mind.

Only with the Renaissance were major advances made. There were the anatomical sketches of Leonardo da Vinci (1452–1519) with a tripartite ventricular system of the brain, the much more detailed plates of Andreas Vesalius (1514–64) of the cerebral convolutions and their blood vessels, and finally in 1628 William Harvey's description of the circulation of the blood.

René Descartes as a young man.

René Descartes (1596–1650) is of course the intellectual landmark in this field in the first half of the seventeenth century. In his discourse he states: 'As theological errors go there is none more powerful in leading feeble minds astray from the straight path of virtue than the supposition that the soul of brutes is of the same nature as our own.'

Descartes proposed that animals were automata. In relation to his dualistic hypothesis on humans, he was challenged on some crucial grounds by his pupil, the seemingly redoubtable Elizabeth of Palatine. Steven Walker of Birbeck College, London, who has written an outstanding book entitled *Animal Thought*, suggests that her criticisms applied to Descartes and to any subsequent version of dualism. In essence they were:

If an immaterial and purely mental structure is assumed to receive input from the physical body and in turn react and alter the course of physical events in the body, this interface presents a group of problems.

1 How can real matter, atoms and molecules, be pushed and pulled about by something, the mind, that by definition is not part of the physical world?

2 How does the non-material object, the mind, gain information from the physical world while being quite separate from it?

3 If one were to allow the mind to get messages from the body, how can it so entirely be the victim of a great variety of body conditions, intoxications, etc.?

I discussed this issue with Sir John Eccles.

DD:  Elizabeth appears to have accepted the possibility that an immaterial mind might conceivably observe a material world. But it was a problem as to how the mind or soul, which had no physical dimensions or properties, could operate the brain or cause physical or voluntary actions.

Well now, Descartes suggested the soul moved the body like gravity moves lifeless objects, and Elizabeth suggested back to him that that wasn't a terribly good analogy, in that they are both physical entities, and Descartes actually agreed on that—he thought it a poor simile.

Princess Elizabeth then asked if the soul possesses all the power and the habit of correct reasoning, why are these powers so disturbed by an attack of the 'vapours'? Now this rather focuses that consciousness is determined by physical states of the brain, it being much upset by alcohol and hallucinogens, rather than that a separate mind perceives and acts through the brain. What do you feel about that?

JE:  Well, of course, it's so simple. I know something

very much more than those people in the past about the brain. And what I say is this, and this is what I have been proposing in my recent hypothesis, that the mind is able to work on the special ultra-micro sites of the brain under special conditions—this is the cerebral cortex through the microsites of operation. You go down to the detailed structure now, and I can't describe it to you. There are micro structures so small that they are in the range of quantum physics operation. The quantum physicist Henry Margenau started me off on this. The actual mass of the particle, $10^{-18}$ grams, is all that is required to open the transmission from a synaptic vesicle. Can the mind using quantum physics, working through quantum physics, affect such a minute structure in the brain? This is the proposal: that at that level of mass, you can do it by energy, borrowing and pay-back. It's all described. [See chapter 7.]

DD:   But allowing the mind is separate and could do that, why should it be chemically deranged by intoxication of the brain. As J.Z. Young says, 'I'm nothing without my brain.' If it is transcendental . . .

JE:   I agree with that, but of course that's all you'd expect. You are working on an instrument, the brain. And if the instrument is out of order a bit, then of course what you are thinking and demanding and so on, your mind's influence on the brain is correspondingly deranged.

DD:   If it does have a lot of alcohol it's not a matter of your speech being slurred—in other words, the physical motor mechanisms of the brain being deranged? The point is what you're thinking about—that is, the quality of that superb instrument—is to an extent deranged by the chemical events in the body. This is one example.

JE:   Yes, because it's both ways. You are going from the brain to the mind, the mind to the brain, and if the brain is disturbed then the mind is disturbed, etc. It all works completely. People misunderstand the situation. One has really to face up to this story because there are the identity theorists, like you're describing now, who believe that the mind is only a special aspect of the brain performance but they've never shown how it does it. What is this special aspect? It's just a hypothesis by Feigl, for example, and it's quoted and quoted but never tested. Then as regards the way in which one talks about the mental world, the world we live in, you have to do more than small and simple movements. You've got to think of the whole of your mental life, and we live in this mental world. You don't know about your brain at all, but you do know about your mind and thinking and experiencing and loving and caring and fearing and enjoying. Furthermore, and this is a strange thing, people don't realise that there's no colour in the matter/energy world—only wavelengths. The colour is made in the mind . . .

DD:   Many other sensations . . .

JE:   All the senses. Everything is made in the mind. How are you going to explain that? How do we come to think of something being red, or green, or whatever. We know how it all happens in the physical world, but it only stays in the end in the brain as impulses, not as experience. All experiences are in the mind, and that is where we are committed, really for our whole life, not to matter–energy world being prime, and the brain–mind world secondary. Actually it is the mind

world that's primary. We only know about the matter–
energy world through our perceptions—it comes into
our mind. We think about it that way, so we are really,
you see, almost a spiritual monist—Bishop Berkeley!

* * *

Recently Sir John Eccles has stated that an appealing
analogy is to regard the body and the brain as a superb
computer built by genetic coding. The soul or self is
the programmer of the computer. It is our lifelong
intimate companion, with all the implications of Chris-
tian theological belief with liberation from the body.

However, it seems to me there is still the need to
face the fact that the stream of consciousness is determined by the physical state of the brain—be it
deranged by the action of amphetamine, alcohol or
high fever—rather than it is that an autonomous mind
perceives and acts via an instrument, the brain. If
there is an immaterial reasoning process completely
separate from the body, how is it deranged by a few
glasses of wine? If the mind is a pilot or driver, then
if the car machinery goes wrong it might prevent the
steering but should not incapacitate the driver. But
brain malfunction can upset every subjective experience and every mental capacity, and as blood chemistry goes awry the whole structure of rationality and
intellect may crumble.

## AN ASIDE ON REFLECTIONS OF THE GREEKS PERTINENT TO PRESENT-DAY DEBATE IN THE UNITED STATES AND AUSTRALIA ON GOAL-DIRECTED RESEARCH

When browsing through ancient literature, one cannot help but be struck as to how apposite some of the issues debated then are to the arguments that wax and wane in Australia on the issue of research today.

Plato and Aristotle both held that the pursuit of knowledge was an end in itself. Aristotle says:

> For it is only to their wonder that men now begin and at first began to philosophise . . . Therefore, because they philosophise in order to escape from ignorance, it is evident they are pursuing knowledge in order to know, and not for any utilitarian end.

It is also true that for ordinary people, as Geoffrey Lloyd points out, what counted was the practical utility of the inquiry. In Plato's *Republic*, during discussion about the education of the guardians and whether astronomy should be included in their education, Glaucon says: 'I certainly agree. Skill in perceiving the seasons, months and years is useful, not only to agriculture and navigation, but also just as much to military art.' But Socrates replies: 'I am amused that you seem to be afraid lest the many suppose you to be recommending useless studies.'

One group of society for whom the contemplative life was not the main motive was the doctors. Their investigation of the body and scientific research was partly to satisfy their curiosity, or 'owing to their wonder', as Aristotle puts it. But their theories were of more than academic interest to their patients. The aim of their treatises was practical ideas. Aristotle says of medicine:

It is an art which all men use on the most important occasions in which they honour, especially in the person of those who are good craftsmen and practitioners in it. For some medical practitioners are bad, others far superior: this would not be the case if there were no such thing as medicine or if no research or discoveries had been made in it, but all would be equally inexperienced and ignorant in it, and the treatment of the sick would be entirely a matter of chance.

And, in regard to research itself, of great contemporaneity is Galen's quote of Erasistratus:

Those who are completely unused to enquire are in the first exercise of their mind, blinded and dazed. They straightway leave off the enquiry from mental fatigue and an incapacity that is no less than of those who enter races without being used to them. But the man who is used to enquiry tries every possible loophole as he conducts his search and turns in every direction, and so far from giving up the enquiry in the space of a day, does not cease his search throughout his life. Directing his attention to one idea after another that is germane to what is being investigated, he presses on until he arrives at his goal.

# 3

# Consciousness in animals

In the Gifford lectures given in Edinburgh in 1972 and 1973, the physicist Longuet-Higgins proposed:

> The idea of a goal is an integral part of the concept of mind, and so is the idea of 'intention'. An organism which can have intentions, I think, is one which could be said to possess a mind ... To form a plan and to make a decision—to adopt the plan. The idea of forming a plan in turn requires the idea of forming an internal model of the world.

In this chapter we are going to focus on the issue of consciousness in animals. I will take the view that there is an evolutionary continuity and that features we know exist in humans have their origins in early life forms.

In proposing continuity, there is inherent an idea of progress and increase of powers, but one may wonder whether different types of consciousness emerged independently at different stages of evolution. The idea of convergent evolution embraces the fact that powerful selection pressures have caused many different animals to develop the same type of capacity to adapt to the life circumstances or utilise an advantage.

That is, the convergence arose because of the big dividends accruing to development of the adaptations and not as a result of common ancestry. Classic examples are the development of different types of eye in different species—for example, octopus versus man— or the convergent evolution of flying by insects, birds and bats. Perhaps it is possible that as larger aggregates of neurones occurred in the evolution of different animals, this convergent process in neural masses of sufficient size gave rise to differing conscious processes? Maybe in primitive nervous systems, for example, if some dim awareness exists, there is a great limitation on or no cross-matching of information from different senses—giving a quite different circumstance of perception to that extant in the higher mammals. Possibly the advantage accruing from cross-matching of different types of sensory inflow to give a coherent picture was a powerful pressure for the emergence of awareness.

There is a gradient from what may be proposed as simple perception in lower forms up to the zenith, which is human mental capacity and language—this last being a wholly spectacular advance over the brains and capacities of other hominoids, the great apes.

The great apes are able to use symbols and learn and use sign language of the type used by deaf people (American sign language), but as Sir John Eccles points out there is little or no attempt by them to use this capacity to ask questions about the outside world in any effort to understand it. The three-year-old human has a torrent of questions. Apes use the sign language entirely pragmatically, including expression of desire. Dr Herb Terrace, of Columbia University, who studied the chimpanzee Nim Chimpsky, doubted if any utterances were spontaneous, and proposed from video records that they were whole or partial imitations of the teacher's most recently signed utterances.

Another way of looking at it is that some animals, particularly the higher apes, may be quite good at times at problem-solving, but creating problems and indeed on a grand scale is almost peculiarly a human attribute. Some would say too much so.

> What a piece of work is a man!
> How noble in reason! how infinite in faculty!
> in form, in moving, how express and admirable!
> in action how like an angel! in apprehension
> how like a god! the beauty of the world!
> the paragon of animals!
>
> (*Hamlet*, II.ii.)

St Thomas Aquinas in the thirteenth century was considerably more charitable to animals than Descartes, suggesting 'The sensitive power of animals are conscious within themselves.' He also suggested that the powers of humans are not so different from those in animals; they are only heightened. Correspondingly, in thinking of animals' souls Aquinas believed they were immortal. We can recall that when St Mael, who was very short-sighted, baptised the penguins in Anatole France's *Penguin Island* (1908), St Catherine, God's Counsellor in this difficult situation, suggested that the solution of the ecclesiastical dilemma was to give them a soul—but a small one.

Dr Jacques Monod of the Collège de France, like Charles Darwin, seems to have little doubt that simulation, or forming images of the future, is not an exclusively human function. The puppy showing its joy at seeing its master getting ready for the daily walk obviously imagines—that is, anticipates—the discoveries it is about to make. Later it will simulate the whole thing again, pell mell, in a dog's dream (a matter we will address further on).

Professor W.H. Thorpe, the distinguished Cambridge zoologist, states that we can never say with certainty that any piece of behaviour in animals, however elaborate and however much it suggests the presence of consciousness, cannot possibly be the unconscious result of a physiological mechanism. The solipsist position is that we can only really know consciousness in ourselves—an apparently impregnable position. Bertrand Russell remarked that he was cured of solipsism for life by receiving a letter from a woman saying, 'I'm so glad you think there may be something in solipsism. I wish there were more of us.' Thorpe believes that solipsism is at least refutable to the extent that nobody believes it.

I put the pivotal question of consciousness in animals to Dr Miriam Rothschild, Sir John Eccles, and Dr Donald Griffin. Dr Rothschild prefaced her answer to me by emphasising the different and sometimes superior capacities of some sense organs of animals and how this might mislead one into interpreting their actions in a human vein. This sector is recorded in the transcript at the end of the book.

*Discussion with Dr Miriam Rothschild*

DD: In terms of the issue of a plan or an intention, to what extent have you seen that in your animals?

MR: I have lived very closely with dogs for about fifty years, and I can only think of three separate instances where one felt that the dog had a plan and anticipated your behaviour before it occurred. I had a Shih tzu who was very fond of walking, but when it got old it couldn't go for long walks. It had rheumatism and so forth. When I left the house it used to come as far as just in front of the steps where one went out of the house and it used to sit down and watch the direction I took. Then it would take a short cut so that it arrived at the destination or nearly the destination where I was going; and it was very interesting how it had watched carefully which way I was going. This dog had very long hair. As you know, Shih tzus are very small, they are like a Pekinese, rather near the ground. And it really didn't like walking through long grass or getting wet. I took a certain direction to a cottage that was over the hill. It would brave the long grass so that it could intercept me at a certain point.

DD: It had an expectation, in your view, as to where you would appear.

MR: Oh, yes. Although it was out of sight of the house, it would take the appropriate short cut. That was one of the very impressive incidents of the dog thinking ahead. Then the other one, which was perhaps even more extraordinary, was this question of the dog's preference for certain chairs to sit on. Now, I had a very large, heavy, rather dumb labrador, but once it took the dogs' favourite chair it was too large for the collies to dislodge, and one of the highly intelligent collies used to go when he wanted to get into this chair, fetch a ball, drop it in front of the labrador. Instantly he was tempted to jump off and catch the ball, and the collie would take the chair. I have thought now of another episode with the same collie: I was writing at my desk in my nightgown, in my bedroom, when the collie came scratching at the door. I opened the door, and the dog was obviously agitated and intimated to me—I got the idea it wanted to go out into the garden and pee—so I got up, and obviously there was something different because the dog caught hold of my nightgown and pulled me to the door, something it had never done before, and I followed the dog. I was so interested in what it was up to. It went straight along to my daughter's room, where she was being violently sick, and this was a really very curious episode, and that seemed to be a very intelligent act.

DD:  Had that happened before with your daughter?

MR:  Never. My daughter, who had broken her back and was in a plaster cast and therefore could not help herself at all, was immobilised in the bed vomiting. And the dog came into my room and drew my attention to this fact, and actually picked up the end of my nightgown in its mouth and pulled me along. That I thought was a very extraordinary episode. And with all my ideas of cues of things, I couldn't make that fit in, except that the dog really knew that my daughter was distressed and wanted in some way to attract my attention.

\* \* \*

*Discussion With Sir John Eccles*

DD:  Jack, in the dialogue between Sir Karl Popper and yourself in the book *The Self and its Brain*, Popper proposes that if the evolutionary story applies to life and consciousness there ought to be degrees of life and consciousness. He elaborates that theme. As I recall in the discussion at that time, in terms of consciousness in animals, it was about 1977, you mentioned that you had something of an agnostic view on that. Now, would it be correct that your position has changed quite a bit, as it often does in science? You have written in 1988 that 'There can be no doubt about the mental experience of domesticated animals, dog, cat and horse', and you say 'I feel the play of young animals is a convincing criterion of consciousness, as also curiosity and the display of emotions, in particular the evidence of devoted attachment.' So you appear now to be in no doubt about the conscious processes in animals.

JE:    Oh, yes, I am. It is quite true I have changed. I was always, though, thinking 'how can we test?' And there is no test of this at all.

DD:    They can't tell you ...

JE:    That's right. You see, I can believe that you are conscious now because we can talk in language, we know the use of words, and we can, as it were, have any level of discussion on this question. You can't do that with an animal at all. The only way to know, say, if a dog is conscious is to be a dog! That is the way you might say.

DD:    Would you infer from intentions, though, if they appear to have a plan and, of course, expectations?

JE:    Oh, yes, that is the way I do it. So I am quite orthodox in this respect. I distinguished so much between consciousness and self-consciousness.

\* \* \*

*Discussion With Dr Donald Griffin*

DD:    We have all considered Longuet-Higgins' criterion of a creature having a mind if there is clearly evidence of intention or future plan which bespeaks the formation of images, an internal model of the world. On these grounds, a remarkable animal is the beaver. Obviously it is genetically programmed, it is instinctive that it builds dams and constructs lodges. I gather there is good evidence though that it is anything but only an automaton in terms of action if the dam is breached or interfered with in any way.

DG: Yes, they do repair dams that have been damaged. Perhaps the most striking case though, a situation in which it is very hard to explain what they do in terms of a rigid genetic programming, is that quite often, but not invariably, when one of their ponds has been frozen solid in the winter for a long time with a thick layer of ice over it, what the beaver do is cut holes in the dam and lower the water level. This is of course exactly the opposite of building the dam. The advantage to the beaver is not altogether clear, but one possibility is that it allows them to swim about in the pond and breathe air under the ice of frozen ponds without having to hold their breath. They do swim around under the frozen ponds to get to food stores or to get to places where the water is open and they can go outside. But in general, I think, the behaviour is both fascinating and highly suggestive. I would like to stress that I think this whole area of animal consciousness—what animals think and feel—is not an area we know enough about to be at all positive or dogmatic. It's a scientific area of unknowns and uncertainty. Many scientists are very uncomfortable dealing with it at all. It's an almost taboo area for those scientists who study animal behaviour. And the reason usually given is that while animals may have conscious thoughts it is said that there is no way in which we can ascertain what, if anything, they are thinking or feeling.

DD:   They can't tell you?

DG:   Well, I believe they can. That's my special approach to this subject. And we are getting away from the beaver for the moment—I'll come back if you like. But it seems to me that animals communicate a great deal with each other and sometimes with other species. It is like pets communicating with their masters, and animal communication does provide us some evidence, not perfect, or 100 per cent conclusive evidence, of what the animal is thinking—if it is communicating its thoughts, as it may well be. So my answer to the objection they can't tell us is, perhaps, they can tell us if we would only listen.

Now beaver do many other things that are quite suggestive of versatile behaviour that is not something that you can readily imagine having been developed in the course of natural selection. For example, in captivity beaver have been observed to build things that they don't ordinarily build in nature in order to get at something they want. For example, the French student of animal behaviour, Richard, had an enclosure for beaver. These were cutting down the trees, and he wanted to keep some trees for shade, so he put a very heavy iron grille around the trunks of some of these trees. But the beaver piled up mud and sticks and branches around the trunk of the tree until they could get above the grille and proceeded to cut the tree in the normal fashion.

DD:   A bit like Koehler's chimps, and putting boxes on top of one another to get at a banana.

DG:   It is quite like that. Of course, beaver do pile up stuff for other purposes. It isn't quite as novel behaviour as a chimpanzee picking up a box and putting it on top of another box. They do a lot of piling up of stuff. The point is they don't ordinarily pile up stuff around trees. They just go and start biting with their very wonderful sharp teeth at the bark, so here they were applying a sort of behaviour they would normally use for building dams or building lodges to this problem of getting up above the iron grille that they couldn't bite through. In another similar experiment, Richard built a platform a metre high, and these were captive beaver that were eating food that he had provided. They were eating bread, which they liked, and he put a loaf of bread on top of this platform a metre up off the ground where the beaver couldn't reach it. The pole was an iron pipe that they couldn't chew through. So they piled up material around this pipe in order to get up to the platform and get the bread. They do a number of things like that sometimes—not always.

Other captive beaver, studied in Switzerland by Aeschbacher and Pilleri, proved very ingenious at cutting little pegs with their teeth to put in the holes in pipes through which the water was escaping from their tank. This caused the water to flood and made an emergency for the people running the laboratory. Beaver don't ordinarily cut little things and put them in holes in pipes. But in this situation where the water was running out, some of them developed this new sort of behaviour that was appropriate to their purposes, which was to raise the water level. It wasn't the purpose of the human managers at the laboratory.

DD:   I understand a few things have been done like that with dams, like putting pipes through at a right angle to the dam in order to drain the pond, and beavers have actually, even though there have been holes in the pipe along its length, have actually plugged those holes. My friend Dr Haber of Harvard

University told me about this in one pond on his property. They have actually pushed dirt into the bottom end.

DG:   Yes, that is a common technique that people use when they have beaver flooding places they don't want them to flood but don't want to kill the beaver. They put a pipe through the dam, and the entrance to the pipe is several feet upstream and underwater, and there are lots of holes. Usually this works. Usually the beaver don't manage to plug all the holes, and the water running out of the pipe below the dam is of course making a lot of noise. If the beaver just pile stuff where there is a lot of running water, they ought to do it there. They may to some extent, but usually this works. On the other hand, in some cases, beaver do manage to find the holes and plug them even if they're several feet above the dam.

DD:   That implies it is not a sort of a simple fixed action pattern, which is released by the sound of running water. It will do it on the side where there is no running water?

DG:   Yes, that's right. And this business, the sound of running water, is certainly one important factor in stimulating dam-building and repair of the dam after the damage. But when you watch where beaver are building dams, often they will start a dam in a place where the water is not running and making nearly as much noise as another place a few feet away. If they went around piling stuff wherever the water was running the most noisily, they wouldn't get an effective dam; they'd get a lot of piles of stuff here and there where the ripples in the stream were. They don't do that. I think that is typical of the simplifying explanation that scientists tend to go for—finding, for example, that if you do play back the sound of running water, beaver will often pile stuff on the loudspeaker. So they say 'Ah ah, the stimulus to dam-building is the sound of running water', but they don't stop to realise that this is only one factor.

DD:   Right. Well, perhaps one of the more suggestive lines of evidence of self-awareness in animals is the process of imitation. This presumptively involves the capacity to copy a novel or improbable act for which there is no instinctive tendency. Presumably there must be some image of its own body in order to electively contrive that it mimics accurately the acts of another creature. I wonder what your view is on this in relation to mimicry observed in dolphins? They are not, obviously, Laurence Olivier, but the reports are rather remarkable.

DG:   They are, some of them. Again, it's not every dolphin under every situation, but in some studies of captive dolphins they've shown a remarkable versatility of imitation. Tayler and Saayman in South Africa studied some bottle-nosed dolphins, the common one which is mostly used in captive aquariums and in shows. They found that these dolphins were imitating other aquatic animals that were in the tank—seals and sea turtles—the swimming and postures that weren't normal for a dolphin but were normal for the seal or the turtle. When divers went into the tank to clean the windows and do other things, the dolphins seemed to be imitating them, in two ways. One, picking up in their mouths little pieces of something and scraping the bottom the way the man had been scraping with a brush. And also making sounds that were similar to the bubbling of air out of the divers' breathing apparatus.

DD:   Did it actually blow bubbles?

DG:   I don't know how they made the sound, but they made sounds that sounded similar to those made by the diver. Dolphins have a very complicated sound-generating system—they can pass air back and forth between different parts of the tract, their respiratory tract—so I don't know how these sounds were made, but they could easily do it without actually emitting air from their blow-holes.

DD:   Well, it might be argued that sound mimicry is perhaps not as complex as a train of body movements uncharacteristic of the usual behaviour of the species. However, we have the lyrebird in Australia, which has an extraordinary repertoire ...

DG:   Could I back off to the dolphins, because I was going to mention another case which is much more like what you suggested: imitating bodily movements. Lewis Herman in Hawaii describes in one of his books some dolphins that had been in a tank together, two or three of them. And one, but only one, had been taught some rather complicated trick. I remember, it was grasping a ball to which a rope was attached, swimming with the ball and pulling something and then maybe jumping through something. I don't remember the details. But only this one dolphin was trained to do this trick, and the others never did it. They couldn't have done it and they weren't observed because it required that people provide the apparatus. This dolphin was then removed, and one of the others immediately went through the whole business, did the whole trick except she did it somewhat differently, poking the ball with her nose instead of grasping it in the teeth, but all the rest of this rather complicated and, for a dolphin, abnormal behaviour. Then that one either got sick or died. It was removed. The third one—I think there may have been more than three but I am sure about this one, which had been in the tank observing all along but never doing it—immediately took over and did the trick but in the way the first dolphin did it, grabbing the ball in its mouth and swimming. So those dolphins must have been watching their companion and must have had some idea of this whole, rather complicated trick but had never done it themselves. Suddenly the situation was appropriate, and they did it all quite accurately.

So that it would seem to me that they must have had some simple awareness of what this acrobatic procedure was—though I would want to emphasise that we don't know any way of absolutely proving such inferences that these dolphins were thinking about the trick they had learnt by observation. You can always argue that they just learned it but they never thought consciously about it, but it seems to me it gets less and less plausible to suppose that—when the animal does something as complex and versatile and as different from anything that it ordinarily does as these dolphins imitating this complex tricky behaviour.

DD: Going through a sequence of motor performances like that, it must imply, or could imply, a body image of the animal. I mean, in order to imitate?

DG: You would think so. It is hard to imagine doing it without thinking about either—perhaps not every muscle contraction—but 'I will swim', 'I will grab that thing with my mouth' or 'I will poke it with my nose'. It is hard to see how an animal could, if it thinks about things at all, how it could avoid thinking about its own actions, which are a very important part of its life.

* * *

## THE ABILITY TO LEARN

Neurophysiologists and neuroanatomists have discovered no functional or structural differences in the nerve cells and synapses (the transmission system between nerve cells) of humans and animals. Of course, there are large differences between the overall anatomy and organisation of the human brain and that of apes and lower animals. Notably, for example, there is the lack of development of the special brain-surface areas devoted to speech in apes and lower animals, although Geschwind and LeMay of Harvard University have shown cortical asymmetry in apes, and a well-marked long Sylvian fissure across the temporal lobe, which Adrian Desmond, author of *The Ape's Reflexion*, notes marks out the human language area, and the region in the ape compares favourably with humans. The surface of the frontal lobe in humans is almost double what it is in apes, and fourfold the area in dogs. The virtual absence in an orangutan, for example, of the cortical areas that become specialised for human language is, as Eccles points out, 'The probable explanation of the inability of the apes to learn language at the human level.'

The areas subserving the process are developed in each person before birth. Thus, congruent with considerations that children of all races are equally well equipped with the ability to learn any human language and Noam Chomsky's idea that there is a universal grammar, it follows that the structure of grammar may reflect the micro-organisation of the linguistic areas of the brain. As with other instinctive behaviours, a signal feature is that not only is some behaviour pre-programmed, there is also programmed the propensity (or facilitated ability) to learn behaviour relevant to the basic elements that are genetic.

This is obvious as an overwhelming feature revealed in studies of innate behaviour controlling, say, ingestion. An animal depleted of a particular nutrient is often good in a cafeteria situation at finding the substance it needs on its first experience, but it is usually much better on a later occasion. In another context, if an animal takes a new food and is poisoned and made sick (even if the onset of the sickness is four to eight hours later), it has a remarkable ability to associate its sickness with what was eaten hours before. It will forever after refuse that food. This reveals the animal's propensity to learn. The nerve pathways are genetically wired so as to specifically associate sensory inflow from taste and smell of the sickmaking object eaten with the gut consequences and attendant nausea-producing sensations even though they develop some hours later.


LEVELS OF CONSCIOUSNESS

Two different levels of consciousness have been recognised by many scientists and philosophers who have pondered the issue. The first level, perceptive consciousness, is the state of being immediately aware of something, events or relations. It is, in this sense, tied to the present. But it is not confined, because the past can be remembered and the future imagined. However, a sufficient ratification for being conscious at a particular time is that one can remember afterwards what was going on at that time. *The Oxford English Dictionary* gives the definition of consciousness as 'the totality of the impressions, thoughts and feelings which make up a person's conscious being'. Overall, then, there is a level of consciousness that can be termed 'perceptual awareness' or 'perceptive conciousness'.

We can contrast this with the higher-level 'reflective awareness' which embodies the idea of being aware of one's perception and thoughts and thus one's own existence—the inward turning of consciousness we referred to earlier. It is a higher level than simply perceiving the present—although it is obvious that being aware of the present is anything but simple. Whether perceptual or reflective, it can be argued in terms of evolutionary continuity that an awareness that allows the existence of internal images of the outside world which can be compared with present sensory input could confer great survival advantage.

Now, facing up to the issue of the actual evidence as to whether animals are conscious, it is challenging to take the hardest question first: Is there self-awareness in animals, at least in the higher species? We should also look at one very stringent criterion, which is whether there is any evidence that animals might be aware of their future death. In the maturation of the human brain, knowledge or recognition of self by a child looking at a mirror antedates by several years any awareness of death.


MIRRORS AND SELF-AWARENESS

Mirrors have a peculiar fascination for humans and animals alike. They have been used by people for more than 3000 years. Many animals, when confronted with their reflection in the mirror for the first time, react as in the presence of another animal of the same species. This behaviour has been ingeniously studied by Dr Gordon Gallup, of the State University of New

York. He remarks that the behaviour of an animal can, and frequently does, serve as a signal and thus stimulation of another animal. Aggressive displays by animals as varied as fish, birds, sea lions and primates towards their reflection in a mirror has been observed, and presumably the crucial issue of reinforcement resides in the fact that the image appears to respond aggressively to them. It is known that a bird may fight its image in a hub cap to exhaustion. Consistent with the fact that a mirror image has the same psychological significance as another organism, it has an enhancing effect on the amount of food eaten by a chicken as the actual, competitive presence of a member of the same species would have. The enhancing effect on egg-laying and ovulation in pigeons and doves has also been observed.

Animals as well as human infants may try to look behind a mirror when presented with a reflection of themselves, fortifying the notion that a reflection is interpreted as representing another individual. Thus a mirror elicits behaviour directed at another member of the same species (a conspecific) and in the laboratory can be used to study visually induced and visually guided social responses. Other variables, such as smell, are eliminated. With a visually competent human being, the behaviour is self-directed; the reflection is used to inspect personal features and respond to them.

In birds, not only does mirror-image stimulation elicit aggression as towards a conspecific entering the existing social hierarchy, but reflection sometimes acts as a supranormal stimulus. For example, a reflection is better than a live companion in reducing the distress calls made by a chicken temporarily separated from its brood-mates.

This other-animal-directed behaviour towards a reflection, as shown by animals, could be seen as a discontinuity from the human. The age at which a child recognises itself in a mirror is somewhat controversial. It may not be until twenty months of age. Verbal indications of a stable self-concept with use of self-reference pronouns or the individual's name do not appear until about two years of age. People born with congenital visual defects, which are eventually corrected, not only respond initially after the operation for restoration of sight to a reflection as if it were another person, but also reach for reflected objects. Mentally retarded children may show prolonged response to reflection as if to another person. Psychotic people often cease to recognise themselves, and may behave as if to another, and reach behind a mirror.

Gallup's experimental work on chimpanzees is of remarkable interest. He studied four pre-adolescent male and female wild-born chimpanzees, which were reared as a group. Each was put by itself for eight hours a day in a room empty except for a mirror placed in front of the cage. Over a period of ten days a clear-cut behaviour change was seen. Initially each of them responded as they would to a conspecific rival, with bobbing, vocalising and threats. By three days this social behaviour had waned, and eventually ceased. From three days onwards, self-directed behaviour was seen almost exclusively. That is, there was precise manipulatory access to otherwise-inaccessible information, such as picking bits of food from between the teeth, visually guided manipulation of the anal–genital area, blowing bubbles and making faces with help of mirror feedback, and turning back the lips with fingers to see into the mouth. Animals removed mucus from the corner of the eye or inside the nostril with visual control. The change of the behaviour indicated that the chimpanzee recognised the identity of the reflection.

Kessa, a four-year-old female gorilla at the Centre International de Recherche Medicale, Franceville, Gabon, has her first experience of a mirror in her cage. Over two hours she spent 30 to 40 per cent of the time gazing at the mirror, put her arm up to touch her reflection, put her lips to the mirror often (see smudges on mirror, opposite page) and also put her arm behind the mirror.

To more rigorously define this, each chimp was then anaesthetised, and whilst unconscious an odourless red dye was painted over the eyebrow and on the top of the opposite ear—positions impossible for the animal to see without a mirror. After keeping a careful score of the animal's spontaneous or random touching of areas around the marks in the absence of the mirror during a pretest in the recovery period, Gallup reintroduced the mirror to the cage. Thereupon the number of mark-directed responses—that is, finger-touching of the areas—went up dramatically, more than 25-fold. The chimpanzee then either inspected its fingers or smelled them. If the reflection were interpreted as another animal, the chimp might have reached to the mirror and touched the red of the reflection. But the co-ordinated action of fingering its red-daubed head, guided by the reflection in the mirror, and then examining its own fingers, would seem decisive.

*The issue is that you cannot examine otherwise-invisible portions of your body with the aid of a reflection unless you know who you are—that is, the animal is aware of its self.*

There was a complete absence of behaviour directed towards other chimps on the day, and the time spent looking at themselves in the mirror increased threefold.

As a further elaboration of this inquiry, chimpanzees that had been in the wild and had no previous exposure to mirrors were anaesthetised and the same procedure followed. During first exposure, the red dye was completely ignored, and the behaviour towards the mirror was unmistakably as if to another chimp, indicating that self-recognition with the previous animals was learned during the 80 odd hours of mirror exposure prior to the dye experiment.

With macaque and rhesus monkeys that had fourteen days of mirror exposure, the responses were always as if to another monkey. When the red-dye experiment was carried out, they continued to behave as if their reflection were another monkey. Tests on young cynomologous monkeys, given much longer exposure (256 hours) before the dye test, also failed to produce any self-recognition. This was true, too, of gibbons.

It was found that macaques were able to recognise some dualism in the relation to objects other than themselves. They could recognise the reflection of food—they would turn away from the mirror where it was seen in order to get access. But they never correctly interpreted their own reflected image. Dr Alan Dixson has spent long periods of time watching macaque monkeys in close proximity through one-way mirrored glass and found that even when their heads were shaven and apparatus for brain injection put on it, the reflections in the mirror elicited no recognition by the monkey that there was something attached to itself.

The self-recognition in chimpanzees has been confirmed subsequently in the orangutan, and also in Koko the gorilla.

Gallup's data indicated that the development of self-awareness in the chimpanzee as indicated by mirror experiments was influenced by early experience and was an acquired phenomenon. The idea was that an individual's concept of self could arise only out of social interaction with others. The way other people react to an individual is the primary source of information about self. How did this viewpoint emerge?

Gallup compared young wild-born chimpanzees, kept in groups, with young chimps born in captivity and reared in individual cages allowing minimal visual contact with fellows. The original experiment with

An important contribution to knowledge of brain function of the great apes has been made by Dr Francine Patterson of Woodside, California. Koko, a female gorilla, was exposed to a mirror when one year old. She kissed it, and looked behind it. She made self-directed behaviour towards her mirror image at about the age of four, but, of great interest relative to Gallup's work (see text), did not have gorilla companions until a year later. The photographs show Koko (*above*) using a mirror to inspect a spot on her cheek. She contorts her face to get a better view; again, she uses the mirror (*opposite, top*) to more easily view under her arm; (*opposite, bottom left*) to examine her teeth; (*opposite, bottom right*) to examine her tongue. Marking an area on her forehead with paint caused her to touch this area, visually inaccessible without a mirror, 47 times during a test session, whereas during control sessions without the marking the area was touched an average of once. (Photographs by Ronald H. Cohn, The Gorilla Foundation—see *Gorilla*, Volume 14: No. 2.)

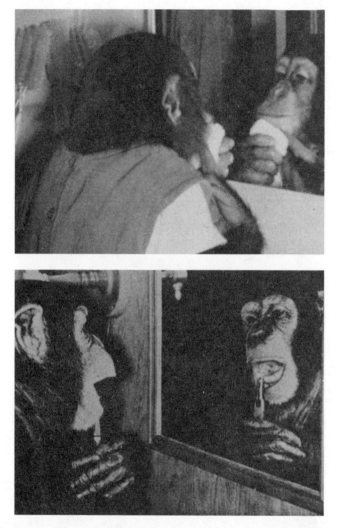

The chimpanzee Vicki was raised from birth by Keith and Catherine Hayes at the Yerkes Primate Laboratory in the manner human children are raised. These photographs by Keith Hayes were published in 1951 and 1954 and show Vicki (*top*) washing her face, and (*bottom*) pulling at a tooth with pliers, both with the aid of a mirror.

initial mirror exposure produced characteristic other-animal-directed behaviour in the wild chimps reared in groups, and then this declined and self-examination began as before. But the ones reared in isolation did not exhibit the social reaction. They spent prolonged times gazing in the mirror but showed no other-chimp-directed reaction, which was not surprising, as they had never had normal social encounters. Gallup noted that prolonged mirror gazing apparently with loss of self-recognition may be symptomatic of impending schizophrenia in humans. Again, the wild animal showed characteristic responses to the dye experiment, whereas the chimps reared in isolation did not show any self-recognition. However, when the isolated chimps were given remedial social experience for twelve weeks by being caged together, they showed development of self-recognition in mirrors.

It is an interesting facet of the self-concept in chimpanzees that those reared in isolation are less impaired in sexual behaviour in later life than those reared by humans. This notion of a self-concept being based on reaction with other members of the species is supported by the case of a chimpanzee, Vicki, raised in a home with humans. When given the task of sorting a pile of photographs into either an animal pile or a human pile, Vicki put her own photograph in the human pile.

I discussed the mirror experiments with Dr Donald Griffin.

DG: I understand that you've talked about the Gallup experiments on indicating self-awareness through mirror recognition. Those experiments have so far worked only with chimpanzees and orangutans and people. People have tried and that experiment has not worked with monkeys and gibbons, so while that is certainly a strong piece of evidence for self-awareness, I am not sure that the absence of doing the mirror trick necessarily means that the animal has no self-awareness. In fact, it is hard for me to see how, if you grant them any, even very simple, awareness of what's going on, how they can fail to have some awareness of what they themselves are doing? It would seem like an awfully important part of the world—if there is going to be any awareness, how can you fail to be aware of your own actions?

DD:   Well, it seems plausible.

DG:   Yes, it's all we can deal with. We can't prove anything in this area.

DD:   Well, it might be argued that sound mimicry is perhaps not as complex as a train of body movements uncharacteristic of the usual behaviour of the species. However, we have the lyrebird in Australia, which has an extraordinary repertoire; it's claimed it can imitate the sound of a sawmill in the bush. One might wonder what goes on in the head of the creature. Presumably there is some sort of feedback audit in the brain whereby it compares the sound it is making with its own memory of what the sawmill or, for example, the kookaburra, sounded like to it. That is, in some way, it would be a critic monitoring and correcting its own performance—perhaps the same basic processes as Joan Sutherland in rehearsal. It seems unlikely, perhaps, it could do this without an awareness of itself and its performance, notwithstanding it obviously has an instinctive drive to sing like other birds and a genetically endowed propensity to mimic the sounds of other birds and its environment.

DG:   Yes, there are other birds. Our mocking birds here in the US do that; they will imitate all kinds of sounds, including human machinery sounds, that they would never hear normally. Many other birds imitate sounds of their companions and there are some dueting birds in India (I have forgotten which species it is) where the mated male and female have a complicated song in which each one sings certain parts, and when one is absent the other one will fill in the parts that the mate normally sang. It would seem to me that they have to be thinking about this other bird when they're doing something like that—though, as always, one can't really prove it in an absolute sense.

* * *

THE DAWN OF SELF-AWARENESS

When addressing the question of self-awareness being synthesised during development—that is, the ego being progressively synthesised from birth onwards—Lord Adrian, Master of Trinity College, Cambridge for many years, and Nobel laureate for studies on the brain, was particularly interested in Edmund Gosse's account of his own childhood in 'Juvenilia'. Gosse, the English literary historian, had lied to his father and not been found out. He suddenly realised not only that his father was not infallible, but also that there was a secret belonging to Edmund Gosse, and to someone who lived in the same body with him. 'There were two of us and we could talk together. It is difficult to define impressions so rudimentary but it is certain that it was in this dual form that the sense of my individuality now suddenly descended on me.'
  Jean Piaget, the Swiss psychologist and student of child development, was also particularly taken with this account, and notes that the moment the child realised his parents did not know all, he straightway

discovered the existence of his subjective self. Piaget suggests that consciousness of self is not a primitive intuition but results from dissociation of reality—a progression heavily dependent on social factors.

I suspect it is extraordinarily interesting for each reader to interrogate his or her own mind as to whether there is a moment, an instance they recall, when they were first indelibly aware of themself. It could be a crucial instance of what Robert Livingston, distinguished neuroscientist at the US National Institutes of Health, has called the 'now print' phenomenon in relation to memory. Livingston remarks that most people can remember exactly where they were and what they were doing at the instant they heard the news that President Kennedy had been assassinated. The intensity of attention assured a 'now print' outcome. With the vast flow of stimuli through sensory channels that goes on during waking life, most does not reach consciousness or get recorded in memory. The searchlight of attention, and indeed, extremely heightened attention, can cause the 'now print' in memory.

The same searchlight of attention might ensure memory of the crucial event in the early construction of the self ego. The instance in my own early childhood, at about age three, is still dramatically clear. My father owned a factory, and one day brought home a couple of hundred or so small wood blocks of various shapes. In those days, ocean liners were pre-eminent, and I had obviously seen pictures of them. For two to three days I suppose I must have worked in the garden in Tasmania intent on building my liner, but the final moment when I put the gangplank across is a vivid recollection. There was a sense of real joy at something I had done or had made. I recall exactly where the sun was and the scene including the light and shadow across a tree fern nearby, and the exact position of buildings, doorways, etc. It printed out, and I suspect the satisfaction had something to do with a sense of self, perhaps in a small, creative way.

I asked Sir John Eccles about this.

JE:   Now, you might say 'how can you talk about it?' Well, one of the things is that you've done it all yourself, with ontogeny and phylogeny. You see, we live from foetus, babyhood, onwards. The whole sequence of development of the brain . . .

DD:   You synthesise consciousness, in effect from experience.

JE:   Well, what I am talking about is more complicated than that. But we have lived through this. A baby is certainly a conscious being, but you can't talk to it any more than you can talk to a dog to find out if it is conscious. And it is even more so with the foetus. Now, when you go on, when does it happen? When does a human being become conscious from your own memories? I was certainly very conscious before I was a year old.

DD:   How do you know that retrospectively?

JE:   You see, it's interesting—I know from the Melbourne Gas Works. That will shock you! I had an extremely bad whooping cough and I was almost dying with this. Now, one of the treatments was to walk you up and put you over the retorts to breathe the gas emission. You got the most violent secretions and coughing, and so on—and I remember this being done three times to me and I was not a year old. My parents believed that would save my life. Something from Melbourne you see. It used to be done regularly at that time with bad whooping cough.

DD:   So that is embedded in your memory!

JE:   At a year and ten months, my baby sister was born. I can remember the details, coming back that day with my father to meet the doctor who had delivered the child, and being told. But these, you see, were my own experiences. So then, if ever I was a self-conscious being, I was even a self then. And this is what you can all do in your own minds. Think of this coming, and when you have children you can look at this same thing. When they ask questions, then the baby is becoming a child. The use of language brings it in.

\* \* \*

THE QUANTAL JUMP

Results of the many experiments of Gallup, of Lethmathe and Ducker on orangutans, and of Francine Paterson of Stanford on the gorilla Koko, suggest that they made the discovery of a dysjunction or quantal jump in brain evolution. In other primates it is not there, but in at least the great apes the necessary brain development exists. It is at this evolutionary stage that the capacity to synthesise awareness of self is emergent.

George Gaylord Simpson, the US zoologist, has stated that: 'Evolutionary progression of behavior must be accompanied by and cannot proceed slower or faster than correlated changes in the brain.'

Walter Hess, the Swiss neurophysiologist and Nobel laureate, says: 'Only those contents of consciousness can be developed that correspond to the organization of the brain.' In the vernacular, if you haven't got the necessary neuronal machinery, you can't have it. In this crowning instance, we are probably seeing in the great apes the emergence of a genetically determined propensity to learn—an ability to learn to synthesise a sense of self.

Indeed, in brain evolution, this development of self-awareness in the hominoids, starting with the great apes, is followed by bipedal walking (upright posture), and this freed the hands for the next great emergent, which is tool-making. Tool-making is, in the definition of Kenneth Oakley of the British Museum, the criterion of the emergence of mankind and represents the shaping of a material for an imagined eventuality—and, as such, is akin to Aristotle's definition of the artist. It began in the late Pliocene epoch, about two to three million years ago. Then eventually there was the ritual burial of the dead, practised by Neanderthal humans about 70 000 years ago. This speaks of identity with one's fellows in awareness of the ephemeral nature of life and self, and the inevitability of death; the sadness of breaking of bonds; and perhaps the beginning of the making of myths.

Forgive, Oh Lord my little jokes on Thee,
and I'll forgive Thy great big one on me.

Robert Frost


AWARENESS OF DEATH

This brings us to the question posed earlier: do any animals have any awareness of their future death? Walter Cannon, the eminent Harvard physiologist, and subsequently Curt Richter, the great psychobiologist of Johns Hopkins, puzzled over sudden mysterious psychogenic death, such as voodoo death, observed mainly in preliterate peoples. A Brazilian Indian condemned by the medicine man is helpless against his own emotional response and dies within hours. In Africa, unknown eating of a wild hen, which is inviolately banned, may on discovery cause a young man to be overcome with fear and die soon afterwards. Dr Herbert Basedow, anthropologist, of Adelaide, has described bone-pointing in Australian Aborigines, and the enormous and immediate psychic and emotional changes in the individual who has been 'boned'—the person would fret until death. Cannon thought this phenomenon indicative of a level of superstition that left primitive people feeling bewildered strangers in a hostile world. He thought death was caused by an outpouring of adrenaline and overaction of the sympathetic nervous system which serves flight and fight.

Forty years ago, Richter studied the effects of severe stress in domestic and wild rats, the latter being fierce, savage and suspicious creatures captured in the slums of Baltimore. He measured endurance when the animals were put in a swimming tank. (This was a glass cylinder with a jet of water and a collar around it, preventing escape.) A laboratory white rat would swim for up to 24 to 48 hours, depending on the water temperature, and then could be taken out. But the wild rats dived to the bottom and nosed around the tank, then swam around further, surfaced, and mostly died one to ten minutes after immersion. Contrary to Cannon's view, Richter found by attaching an electrocardiogram to the rats that they died with a gradual slowing of the heart—an inhibition transmitted by the vagus nerve from the brain. It was not a sympathetic overactivity. Richter has proposed that the situation with the wild rat was essentially one of hopelessness. The rat literally 'gives up' quite quickly. Support for this interpretation was given by the fact that if very shortly after being placed in the water the wild rat is rescued—taken out—it again becomes aggressive. On a future occasion when put in the tank, it will swim for as long as a domestic rat or longer. The wild rat's recovery after removal from the tank is very rapid over a few minutes. Professor Barnett, a biological scientist at the Australian National University, describes how an adult male rat, if it intrudes into the territory of others and is threatened or only mildly bitten, may die suddenly without any cause evident in post mortem examination.

Curt Richter noted that there are many records in medical practice of people dying suddenly from fright, the sight of blood, hypodermic injection or sudden immersion in water. During the Korean war, unaccountable deaths were reported among soldiers with no evidence of pathology. Montaigne described an instance where friends of a man who had obtained his pardon put a hoodwink on his head while still on the scaffold and read out the pardon, but found him dead when they removed the hood.

It is noteworthy that it is said that a primitive man, when freed from voodoo, recovers almost instantaneously.

Though a matter of conjecture, it seems to me that in the wild rat there is the possibility of 'situational perception'. This could encompass what Richter calls hopelessness. The fact that, if it previously experienced being rescued, the wild creature will swim for 50 to 60 hours, supports the contention of the animal being not only conscious (in the sense of being awake), but also able to make some evaluation of its predicament, based on perception of the situation and past experience (such as that of being rescued). This is akin to people who are shipwrecked swimming for very long periods in the hope of being rescued or reaching dry land. It could be argued that in the rat this is coming close to a sense of its own existence, and an expectation of outcome—plausibly to a sense of awareness in the animal, if not self-awareness. At least the animal's perception of its situation profoundly influenced neural and visceral processes.

Alternatively, one might conceive of the wild rat as an automaton, which is programmed for situational perception; and when the rat receives a constellation of inflow evaluated by the internal computer as there being no exit, then a self-destruction mechanism becomes operative. A further elaboration of the automaton might be a rapid reversal of the program to that determining earlier demeanour, if there were the intrusion of a new input such as that provided by the rescue and removal from the situation; the automaton is reprogrammed thereafter.

The question might well be asked as to what the 'survival' advantage' is to an individual animal of a species to have a reproducible and consistent mechanism of sudden death in specific stress situations where death will be inevitable and eventually occur. It is puzzling. Perhaps if individuals are inept enough to get themselves into near-hopeless situations and thereupon an in-built mechanism terminates them, it ensures that they have no progeny, and this is an advantage to the species. But if the situation is hopeless anyhow, such a mechanism is redundant since the outcome is terminal. Lewis Thomas describes how, when his cat caught a mouse and played with it, even if he rescued the mouse at any stage it always died.


CONSCIOUSNESS IN BEES

Finally, to go to simpler life forms, I discussed the question of consciousness in that remarkable creature, the bee, with Dr Donald Griffin.

DD:   Is a honeybee simply a ganglion on legs? Or is there somebody home?—as this is now of great experimental interest.

DG:   Yes, honeybees have provided us, I think, with some very substantial and significant evidence about the possibility of conscious thinking. We are not used to even contemplating the possibility that an insect might think. But if you examine some of the things that many insects do, they are versatile. They do involve, and require learning. It's not just a matter of a rigid program running off regardless of anything else. But more important in the case of honeybees, they communicate in a symbolic and semantic way about specific things. This was discovered 40 or so years ago by Karl von Frisch in a study of what he called 'dances' that honeybees carry out ordinarily in a dark hive, by which they convey to their sisters, the other worker honeybees, distance, direction and desirability of things. I put it that way—said 'things', without saying what things purposely. Now, this is in the dark. How does a gesture convey direction and distance in the dark? It's a sort of waggling run in which the bee crawls rapidly over the vertical honeycomb surface while swaying the body and the abdomen from side to side in a sort of waggling. It's about thirteen waggles per second. They call these 'dances'. The dancer circles first one way and repeats this waggle run, and then the other way. Now, the waggle run is oriented with respect to gravity, and straight up on the vertical surface in the dark means that, outside, you should fly towards the sun. In other words, there is a symbolism here—the sun is not visible in the dark hive. And other directions, straight down means away from the sun, 90 degrees left means 90 degrees left of the sun. The other worker bees, some of them at least, follow this dancer, feel her, perhaps detect faint air movements or sounds, and somehow they get the information that this is a straight-up dance, and they go out of the hive and they search for whatever it is they are searching for in the direction towards the sun. The length of this waggling run is correlated with and seems to convey the distance. No, these are approximate transfers of information—they are not highly precise—the direction is perhaps plus or minus 15 degrees. The distances may be plus or minus 10 per cent, and the bees use odours quite a bit for finding the exact place that is being signalled. Now, ordinarily this is done for food, for flowers, either nectar or pollen that bees gather from flowers. The scent of the flowers is brought back, and the followers go out and search for a flower of that scent. But the symbolic part is the distance and direction and it works over many hundreds of metres, even up to two or three miles, so that going out and just searching for a particular scent over an area of several square miles would be very inefficient. This dancing is not a rigid thing that happens all the time. It happens only when a forager has come back with something that is badly needed by the colony. They learn what's badly needed by further communication—but let's not get into that.

They do this dancing only when something is badly needed. If the beehive has lots of sugar, they don't dance for sugar at all. Sometimes, however, they dance about other things, such as water when it's hot and they need water to cool the hive by evaporation. But the most interesting example of the versatility of this symbolic communication is at the time of swarming, when roughly half the workers—the workers, of course, are non-reproductive females—and a queen have come out of an old cavity because it's got too crowded. They're outside in the open, a great ball of bees hanging in the vegetation or whatever is available, and it's very important that they find another cavity. In northern climates, like this area, or even in southern Australia, I think, they could not survive the winter without being in some kind of a cavity. So the worker bees that under other conditions might go out looking for flowers go out looking for cavities. They poke around, they find little holes in trees and buildings, they crawl around inside them, they come back and they use the same dance to indicate distance and direction of the cavity. They also indicate desirability of both food and other things by the vigour and intensity of the dance. It's not quite clear yet just what the physical dimensions of this vigour are. One obvious thing is a vigorous dance is repeated over and over again. A less-vigorous dance is perhaps repeated only two or three times. But without getting into that, there is communication of intensity of desirability.

DD: With such versatility, they must have a very complex nervous system.

DG: Yes, and this is a nervous system that weighs about one milligram.

DD: How many neurones in a bee's?

DG: Oh, thousands. It's a complex nervous system, and even though it is tiny compared to ours, when you look at anatomical diagrams it's full of complexity. Hundreds or thousands of neurones and plenty of synapses and plenty of possibilities. Just to go on about this—the most interesting thing of all is that ordinarily in this case of swarming, different scouts will have found different cavities and will be dancing about them giving different messages: 'This way, about so far, for the cavity I found.' Another bee an inch or so away would be dancing about a different cavity. How do they reach a consensus because, obviously, the whole swarm's got to go to one and not split up? There is only one queen, for one thing. So what happens is, there is a two-way communication apparently, and both the dancers and the followers gradually come to be dancing about fewer and fewer of these cavities, and these are the most desirable ones. These are the ones that the dancers were dancing most vigorously about.

DD: Has it been established by marking them that those which have been to one cavity earlier and spoken in favour of it, as it were, now take a different view?

DG: That's another thing. Some studies by Martin Lindauer 30 or so years ago show this, at least, occasionally. No one knows yet how common this is. He marked a bee that had been out to a sort of mediocre cavity and danced about it. She now became a follower of one of her sisters or half-sisters who had come back from a better cavity, and this bee now having followed this more enthusiastic dance flew out to the better cavity, came back and joined in the dancing about it! We don't know whether that is the only or the principal factor going on, but what Lindauer and others have observed is that after a time there is no dancing about the less-desirable cavities. More and more about the better ones—and finally after usually many hours of practically all the dancing having been about that one cavity, then the swarm goes off to it. So there's a reaching of a consensus about a very important matter to bees and it is an entirely new experience for these workers. They only live a few weeks but the swarming may not have occurred for a couple of years, so those particular worker bees have never been through this business before. And it suggests to me that they are thinking something simple like 'a nice big cavity that is dry, doesn't have ants in it, and it's this direction.'

DD: Can you deter them by having ants in it or having it across water, which they don't like either?

DG: I am not sure about the across-water factor. But Thomas Seeley, at Cornell, and Lindauer have studied this, and they do crawl around inside the cavities. And Seeley has used experimental boxes that if he makes the same size but the entrance is rather big, and it's not very dark inside, they are not as enthusiastic. If it is wet, if it is leaky, they're less enthusiastic. If it has ants in it, they are not so enthusiastic. So the quality of the cavity matters and the size. If it's too big or too small they are not enthusiastic. So they do evaluate cavities and convey their general level of suitability through this symbolic dancing.

Now, we talk about the human language being a unique way in which we can determine something at least, if not everything, about each other's thoughts. Here's an animal communication system, which is symbolic in a simple way, and it seems to me plausible, although not absolutely certain by any means, that these bees are thinking something similar to the message that they are communicating.

DD: Yes, it's an extraordinary, interesting story. I suppose that if we propose that consciousness is present in many animal species—birds, dogs and chimpanzees, and maybe even bees—it may have emerged independently in these species as neural organisation increased in complexity. You know, when organisms became many-celled, with organs with different functions subserving the whole body politic or organisation, they evolved hearts to circulate fluids in the internal environment. So, in parallel fashion, we come again to William James' proposition that consciousness is what you would expect in the nervous system grown too large to steer itself.

DG: Yes, steering itself, of course, is a complicated notion, and it is very hard to tell what nervous systems are steering themselves. You could argue that for a central nervous system to steer itself does not require consciousness. I like Karl Popper's formulation that it is enormously more efficient to think about things that might happen and decide which is the one you want, rather than going out and trying them and getting eaten.

DD: All the possibilities...

DG: Not only is it very dangerous, as he says, but your foolish ideas can die in your head. Well, I don't like to use the word 'ideas' for animal thoughts, because I think they are probably simpler than what we ordinarily mean by ideas. But to think about simple possibilities, what's likely to happen if I do this or that, and to try it out in your central nervous system, whether you are a bee with a ganglionic system or an anthropoid ape with a big brain, is obviously much more efficient than going out and trying to eat everything, and seeing which things make you sick.

DD: Yes, perhaps. As one might perhaps imagine consciousness emerged in different situations in animal phylogeny. It doesn't necessary follow that if it developed in honeybees because of their organisation, one doesn't have to go quite a fair way up the evolutionary tree before you get another instance?

DG: Yes, there are obvious advantages to honeybees which I didn't mention. They do live in these large colonies, they are entirely dependent on getting in a lot of food. Other insects are after the same food, and when they find a new source it's very advantageous to get a lot of your sisters out there exploiting it. That's less important perhaps for insects and small colonies. But who knows? I think, as I said earlier, this is a subject that scientists have avoided and not studied to any great extent. So there is extreme ignorance about it, and I think that ignorance could be reduced if scientists would devote some of their ingenuity—so successful in other areas—to this very difficult problem.

* * *

# 4

# Probing the human psyche

As I said at the outset, intense fascination with the workings of the brain and the mysteries of the mind have preoccupied poets and philosophers as much as scientists and doctors. The imprisoned Richard II in solitude says:

> I have been studying how I may compare
> This prison where I live unto the world:
> And for because the world is populous
> And here is not a creature but myself,
> I cannot do it; yet I'll hammer it out.
> My brain I'll prove the female to my soul;
> My soul the father: and these two beget
> A generation of still-breeding thoughts,
> And these same thoughts people this little world
> In humours like the people of this world.
> For no thought is contented.

## ELECTRICAL STIMULATION OF THE BRAIN

Dr Wilder Penfield, the distinguished Canadian neurosurgeon, who was much entranced by Shakespeare's words cited above, has given extensive accounts of his study of fully conscious patients on the operating table, in whom a hemisphere (one side) of the brain has been exposed under local anaesthesia and the surface of the brain has been stimulated with small needle electrodes. In an account of the remarkable studies made by him and his colleagues at the Montreal Neurosurgical Institute, he remarks with perhaps more than whimsy:

> The contempt which intellectuals once had for the barber/surgeon lingers on in the minds of men ... making it difficult for them to accept the findings of any surgeon on a par with scientists. I confess that many of us who are surgeons do operate too much, and think too little, but we face special problems. Without stopping to define consciousness, a brain surgeon must act ... As an experimenter he can only be an opportunist. But on the other hand, disease and accident present to him, from time to time, the most perfect experiments. Then he must be prepared to think as well as to act, and to do both quickly.

Penfield was much concerned with surgery for the treatment of epilepsy. In the course of searching for the local source of fits, he applied gentle electrical current to local points on the brain surface. The brain's surface has no sense of touch or pain, and thus the conscious patient would not know where or when the stimulation occurred.

In the right-handed person, as the French neurologist Broca first determined, the brain area controlling speech is in the left side of the brain (the left hemisphere). Even among many left-handed people, speech is very often processed also on the left side of the brain. Penfield found that applying an electrode to the speech area on the appropriate side blocked the patient's ability to speak. For example, a patient who was being shown a picture of a butterfly and knew he was expected to name it, appeared exasperated but

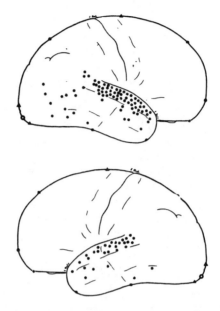

Points of stimulation on the temporal cortex of the brain of conscious patients which produced flashbacks—responses derived from previous experience. (From Wilder Penfield, *The Brain and Conscious Experience* John C. Eccles (ed.), Springer Verlag, Berlin, 1966)

could not speak. Once the stimulus stopped, he could say 'butterfly'. The sensation was rather much that of an idea searching for a word—a sensation many of us have from time to time. The electrode had incapacitated speech, but not interfered with perception and reason.

If the temporal lobe (the lobe of the cortex of the brain beneath the temples of the head) is stimulated on its upper surface, usually one of two events occurs. Either the patient experiences a sudden alteration in interpretation of present experience—what is seen or heard seems suddenly familiar, *deja vu* or *seen before*—

or it is strange and frightening. Alternatively, the patient may have a sudden flashback, an awareness of some previous experience. For example, when the electrode was applied to a particular point, one patient heard a song played by an orchestra which began at a verse and went on to the chorus. She could hum the tune as she was made to hear it. The tempo of humming was what we would expect from an orchestra. The experience could be repeated again and again from the same spot. She could not remember where she heard it. However, another patient who heard a piece of music in a church remembered exactly that it was Christmas Eve in Amsterdam, and she heard the choir and felt again how beautiful it was, even as she lay on the operating table in Montreal. Actually, there had been Canadian soldiers in the church at the time, and she had married one and come to Canada.

From this lobe beneath the temples, the experiences evoked to consciousness have been visual or auditory, or visual combined with auditory. No one has said, 'I am eating or tasting food, or having a sexual experience or a bowel action, or suffering pain.' The outcome from more than a thousand operations is that these psychic experiences have not been evoked from areas of the brain other than this temporal area, which Penfield calls the interpretive cortex—the experience of *deja vu* reflecting the function of interrelation of the present with past experience.

These findings represent the discovery of an anatomical record of the stream of consciousness. When the electrode is removed from the brain surface the psychic experience disappears at once. When the stream of consciousness of a previous period of time is caused to flow again, the electrical excitation follows a pathway through a seemingly unending sequence of nerve cells, nerve fibres and synapses. This involves

down-traffic to the middle brain and then up-traffic to
other regions of the cortex.

The path that Penfield uncovered was formed and
made permanent by neuronal facilitation. A strip of
time seems to run forwards again at time's own normal
pace—that is, real time. The individual becomes
focused once again on matters selected for attention
at that time in the past. Everything that was ignored
then is gone. The emotional element of experience is
retained, whether a fright or a feeling of beauty. What
is preserved is that which Penfield suggests was
illuminated by the searchlight of attention, while the
rest remains in darkness. At any instant, for any one
of us, the flow of sensory information to the brain is
prodigious from all senses—the position of joints, the
viscera, and many other directions—but only some are
selected for attention. And to this the individual adds
his or her own interaction by comparing the present
with the past. A quite selected record of past experience is the result. On the Montreal data, such a record
may or may not be available to elective recall by the
will. Here, electrical stimulation has brought it to the
stream of consciousness. In this regard, in terms of
cerebral and memory organisation, it is fascinating to
read Proust's great classic, *Remembrance of Things Past*:

> With the perturbations of memory are linked the
> intermittencies of the heart. It is, no doubt, the
> existence of our body, which we may compare to
> a vase enclosing our spiritual nature, that induces
> us to suppose that all our inner wealth, our past
> joys, all our sorrows, are perpetually in our
> possession. Perhaps it is equally inexact to
> suppose that they escape or return. In any case if
> they remain within us, for most of the time it is
> in an unknown region where they are of no use
> to us, and where even the most ordinary are

crowded out by memories of a different kind, which preclude any simultaneous occurrence of them in our consciousness. But if the context of sensations in which they are preserved is recaptured, they acquire in turn the same power of expelling everything that is incompatible with them, of installing alone in us the self that originally lived them.

We will return to Proust a little further on, when considering the senses of taste and smell.

At this point, as I have been describing these events, no doubt many readers will recall the entertaining book of neurological case records of Dr Oliver Sachs of New York, entitled *The Man Who Mistook His Wife For a Hat*, and his vivid accounts of patients with damage of various sorts to the temporal lobe. Sachs remarks that, with Penfield's stimulation of a point of the cortex, 'There convulsively unrolls a Proustian evocation or reminiscence.' Dr Sachs, of course, draws a great deal upon Penfield's work in describing them. There was the lady who lived in a home for the elderly, who suddenly had her consciousness continually occupied with songs she had danced to during her childhood in Ireland. The explanation that eventually emerged was that a small stroke had occurred in her right temporal lobe. The songs gradually went away over a couple of months and she reflected afterwards that she did miss them; it was like being given back a forgotten bit of her childhood again, and 'some of the songs were really lovely'. She added, 'It was the healthiest, happiest experience of my life. I can't remember the details now but I know it's all there.'

Dr Sachs also quotes an article in the *New York Times* entitled 'Did Shostakovich have a secret?' A Chinese neurologist, Dr Wang, suggested a metallic shell fragment lodged in the temporal horn of the left ventricle in Shostakovich's brain was mobile. Shostakovich was reluctant to have it removed because, since it had been there, each time he leaned his head to one side he could hear music. His head was filled with melodies, different each time, which he then made use of in composing. X rays allegedly showed the fragment moving around when Shostakovich moved his head. The tentative verdict of the neurologist had been: not impossible!

Dostoevsky, the great Russian novelist, also had some psychical seizures or elaborate mental states at the onset of seizures, and said:

> You all, healthy people, can't imagine the
> happiness we epileptics feel during the second
> before our fit... I don't know whether this felicity
> lasts for seconds, hours, or months, but believe
> me, I would not exchange it for all the joys that
> life may bring.

As well as Penfield's data on surface stimulation, some intriguing facts and observations have emerged in the course of deep exploration of the brain with electrodes while the patient is awake and cooperative. This is during neurosurgical therapeutic manoeuvres for treatment of parkinsonism or for other reasons. Stimulation in a specific area of the thalamus (a great relay station and concentration of nerve cells in the route between the midbrain and the cerebral cortex) can reproducibly cause laughing. The patient volunteers that everything seems funny at the time. It was not the musculature of laughing that was reflexly activated, but the expression of a content of consciousness—sometimes the same amusing situation from former life came to mind.

Dr Robert Heath, a neurosurgeon at Tulane University in the US, has made some remarkable observations on two patients, one being treated for severe mental illness, and the other with intractable epilepsy. Deep-seated electrical stimulation and microinjection of chemicals naturally involved in nerve transmission were used, as well as electrical recordings made from deep in the brain when the patient was conscious. In the female epileptic patient, injections of chemical transmitters on sixteen occasions at weekly intervals in the forebrain or septum caused, after a quarter of an hour, a mild euphoria, and this elevation of mood led to a sexual motive state and repetitive orgasms in another five to ten minutes. In the male patient, stimulation electrically in this same septal forebrain area provided sensations of pleasure, alertness and warmth, with strong sexual arousal. Furthermore, repetition of the procedure over ten days led the patient, who had hitherto been exclusively homosexual, to heterosexual orientation, and subsequently heterosexual intercourse occurred.

Studies by neurosurgeon Sem Jacobsen and colleagues in Oslo have shown that various smell sensations can be evoked by stimulation of deep-seated brain regions. Other neurologists, José Delgado of Spain, and Dr Vernon Mark of Boston and his colleague, Dr Ervin, have shown that uncontrollable violence exhibited by some patients could be set in train by electrical stimulation in the medial part of a structure called the amygdala. It is situated between the midbrain and the cortical grey matter, and coagulation of the nerve cells there greatly improved the life of the patients.

If we put aside from consideration here the matter of medical judgment and the overriding imperative of the patients' interests with any procedure as, for example, such deep-seated brain stimulation and recording, the data, when taken with the outstanding work of

Penfield on local brain-surface stimulation to seek epileptic foci, show a clear fact: The content of the mind or the stream of consciousness can be instantly dictated by a small electrical signal (2 volts), the content of awareness being determined by the place where the stimulus is delivered.

At present there is still an enormous void in our knowledge as to how we can electively, at will, direct the searchlight of our own attention to a particular matter, and so direct the stream of consciousness, yet we do know that simple physical electrical stimulus of some cells on the brain surface can instantly cause a change of consciousness, with a replay incorporating emotional and aesthetic overtones of events long past. The phenomenon is easily physically accessible, as Penfield has shown, even if, in the system of such extraordinary complexity, it is sheer chance as to what will be accessed. In some way, the conscious will can do (usually with precision and accuracy) what the electrode activates at random. The action of the conscious will, as experienced, will no doubt eventually be explained on some matter–energy or material basis, although there will probably emerge quite novel findings compared to what neuroscientists have so far conceived.

## SURGICAL DIVISION OF THE 200 MILLION FIBRES JOINING THE TWO HEMISPHERES OF THE BRAIN—'THE SPLIT BRAIN'

Major discoveries on brain function of high pertinence to our central question have come from the work of Roger Sperry of the California Institute of Technology and his colleagues, particularly Michael Gazzaniga, who now directs a Cognitive Neuroscience Institute in New York. Sperry received a Nobel prize in 1981. Sperry's studies were on patients who, for reasons of treatment of intractable epilepsy, had had severed surgically the 200 million-odd fibres of the corpus callosum—the grand trunk road which connects the two hemispheres of the brain and conducts the traffic between the two sides. Some smaller substructures that join the two sides were also cut. The outcome was that there were now two separate streams of consciousness or knowing within the brain.

The separated hemispheres could sense, perceive, learn and remember independently of one another. In certain circumstances each hemisphere could be oblivious of the cognitive experience or what was known by the other. This has been demonstrated in many ways. When a right-handed patient with thus a dominant left speech hemisphere has had the brain split, if the patient is blindfolded and a familiar object such as a pencil or cigarette is put in the *left* hand, then the mute or subordinate *right* hemisphere connected to the left hand perceives and appears to know quite well what the object is. It cannot express the knowledge in speech or writing, but can manipulate the object purposefully and show how it is supposed to be used. The right hemisphere can remember the object and go out and get it with the same left hand from among an array of objects either by touch or sight. The left dominant speaking hemisphere connected with the right hand, which has not had access to the object, will have no conception of what the object is, and if the blindfolded patient is asked, the speech determining left hemisphere will say so or guess. The subordinate right hemisphere has its own perceptions, reactions and memories. Sperry reports that patients revealed emotional feelings generated by the subordinate right hemisphere, such as a smile on completing

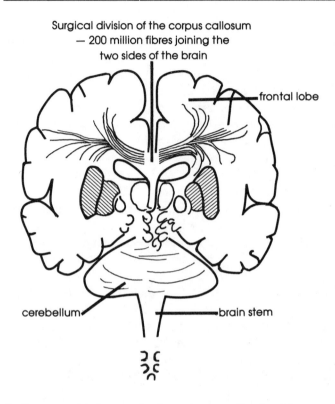

Surgical division of the corpus callosum
— 200 million fibres joining the
two sides of the brain

frontal lobe

cerebellum

brain stem

A diagram of a human brain, cut across the front from side to side (coronal section) showing the division of the corpus callosum consisting of 200–300 million fibres which carry messages between the two sides.

a task with the left hand, or frowning at an incorrect verbal response, or an inept action by the right hand when only the right subordinate hemisphere knows the correct action.

## FREE WILL AND THE SPLIT BRAIN

The question of whether the two disconnected hemispheres each have a will of their own and can get into conflict seemed to arise in the first half of the year after surgery. When a split-brain patient was dressing and trying to put on his trousers, the left hand might start working against the right, and pull the trousers down on that side while the right hand was pulling them up. Or left hand, having helped the right to tie a knot in a rope, might proceed on its own to untie it; the right hand has to supervene. The patient and his wife would refer to 'the sinister left hand', which sometimes would push the wife away aggressively just as the right was trying to get her to come and help with something. Generally, however, there are so many unifying capacities in the brainstem/spinal cord that the functional harmony built in there eventually prevails.

VISION AND THE SPLIT BRAIN

Studies have been undertaken in which two different visual images were fed into the two sides of the brain. This is relatively easily done. It relies on the fact that when you look straight ahead, images from the left side of your body feed (via the optic nerve) into the right side of the brain, and those on the right side of the body feed into the left side of the brain. So if the split-brain patient looks straight ahead, one lot of data goes to the right and one to the left, and it can be arranged that data can be given to only one hemisphere. A picture could be flashed to the left side, and the mute right hemisphere (which receives the information) could pick out the object with the left hand; or if a word were flashed, it could do likewise. When an object was flashed, it could pick out the correct word for it. So the mute hemisphere was anything but stupid, and Sperry remarks that the talking

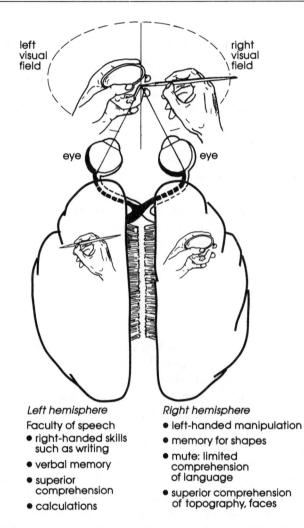

**Left hemisphere**

Faculty of speech
- right-handed skills such as writing
- verbal memory
- superior comprehension
- calculations

**Right hemisphere**

- left-handed manipulation
- memory for shapes
- mute: limited comprehension of language
- superior comprehension of topography, faces

A diagram of a split brain (corpus callosum divided) showing that information coming to the retina from the right visual field feeds by the optic nerve into the left hemisphere, whereas the stimuli in the left visual field feeds into the right hemisphere. The faculties that are dominant or advantaged in the left or right hemisphere of a right-handed person are shown. (Drawn after C. Trevarthen.)

hemisphere knew nothing of these events or the correct answers, and frequently it was necessary to convince the talking hemisphere to keep quiet and let the left hand go ahead on its own, in which case it would usually pick out the correct answer.

For examining the visual field it is possible to divide photographs in half longitudinally and join the faces of two different people, in this way making what is called a chimera. With a central gaze, the left brain sees one face and the right the other. It was found that if the patient is required to match a photograph to what was seen, the experience of the right mute hemisphere dominated. If any linguistic component were involved—that is, if the subject were asked to name the image—the data in the left speech hemisphere dominated. It was also found that the right non-talking hemisphere was ineffectual with arithmetic. But as beautifully described by Gazzaniga in his book *The Social Brain*, it could draw easily with the left hand an object shaped like a cube, whereas the left talking hemisphere was quite inept, notwithstanding that it had the right hand to do the drawing with. Another most interesting result was that if the hemispheres were required to make aesthetic judgments—as when the photographs flashed were of people either beautiful or ugly—the right mute hemisphere was very highly proficient on aesthetics, but the left talking analytical hemisphere could not tell beauty from beast.

## THE BRAIN AS A CONSTRUCT OF MODULES

With the ultimate aim of understanding the function of the normal integrated brain, Gazzaniga has contemplated a number of experimental situations with split-brain individuals. When the word 'walk' was flashed to the right mute hemisphere, the patient responded by pushing his chair back and starting to leave the testing area. The testing was being done in his own home, and when asked what he was doing the patient said, 'I am going into my house to get a Coke.' The left hemisphere was confronted with the task of explaining an overt behaviour initiated not by itself but by the right brain.

In relation to the normal, Gazzaniga reflects that the individual is compelled to interpret real behaviours of his or her own and construct a theory as to why they have occurred. He proposes that the normal individual does not possess a unitary conscious system, but the brain is organised differently. It is not, as Freud suggested, with a conscious and unconscious. Gazzaniga thinks there are a large number of co-conscious modules, and all except one act in non-verbal ways, such that their modes of expression are solely through overt behaviours or more covert actions. (William James suggested that 'The recesses of feeling, the darker, blinder strata of character, are the only places in the world in which we catch real fact in the making.')

Gazzaniga thinks most of these systems, not unlike those existing in animals, can remember events, store emotional reactions to the happenings, and respond to signals relevant to particular memory. All such activities are carried out routinely by cats and dogs, apes and humans. These brain modules in humans are capable of initiating disparate behaviour, and the dominant left hemisphere is commited to the task of interpreting our overt behaviours, as well as the covert emotional responses by separate mental modules of the brain.

There is no philosopher sees

that rage and fear are one disease
Though that one may burn, and this one
  may freeze
They're both like the ague.

These lines from Coleridge touch on a commonplace element in human behaviour. It is sometimes the left cortex's job to rationalise the rage that may have its roots in fear.

Gazzaniga cites other workers whose findings point to the modular notion. Many areas of the brain determine actions that, once initiated, are then interpreted by the left-hemisphere language system, which constructs a theory as to their meaning. The Canadian neurosurgeon Dr Juhn Wada has designed a test primarily aimed at confirming for a surgeon which hemisphere is, in fact, dominant for language. Here we are not dealing with split-brain patients. By way of a catheter put into an artery in the leg and led up to the carotid, supplying one side of the head, a short-acting anaesthetic is quickly injected into that side of the brain. Thus one side of the brain is quickly and temporarily put to sleep. When the test is ready to begin, the patient holds his hands in the air; and when the drug is injected, the hand opposite to the hemisphere which is hit by the drug falls down paralysed. If it is the left hemisphere, the right hand falls, and the left brain no longer understands language. The other hemisphere is awake, and the other hand and motor apparatus are operative. An object, a spoon in this case, was placed in the left hand, and the patient is asked to remember it. It is removed after half a minute. A few minutes later the patient once again regains speech and is asked how he feels. He says 'good' and is told that an object was placed in his left hand. 'Can he say what it was?' He looks puzzled, and denies it; his left talking brain cannot access the information. But when the patient is shown a group of objects, one of which was put in the hand before, he decisively and rapidly picks out the correct object, saying, 'Oh yes, it was the spoon.' As Gazzaniga says, in some way some information was slipped into the brain without the language system being aware. Whatever the explanation, the module with the information does not tell its secret to the language system. Whatever the final explanation of this may be, the experiment shows how information may exist in the brain and can express itself decisively in movement, while at the same time be unavailable to the language system.

I posed some questions on these issues to Sir John Eccles.

DD: Whereas all Western thought underlines the notion of the unity of consciousness and free will, the split-brain data indicate that there can be more than one stream of awareness. Is consciousness a function of neural tissue in action, rather than perhaps a non-material separate entity?

JE: Well, one has to remember where we are about this. At one time, I did take—following even Roger Sperry's experiments—I did take an extreme view. Now my position is that the right hemisphere, separately from the left, is a conscious hemisphere. And it has not only that. It's inherited all the learning procedure, the whole thing. It was part of the combined human brain at one time, and so it has a great deal of memory and ideas built into it, so this is what you're working with, not a naive hemisphere but one that was linked into the brain. The other point I want to make is that it doesn't really act with language in an effective way. Its reactions over emotions can be done by the limbic system which is not cut. There are communications between the two sides of the limbic system. So this can get, as it were, crude emotional reaction across the midline when a section is done on the corpus callosum.

DD:   That reflects, of course, that the right mute hemisphere is possessed of information. It's conscious of something which the talking hemisphere is not.

JE:   Of course, this is certainly the case, and we can really say there are two conscious beings in the one skull. One which is the left hemisphere, which is the talking one, and one which is the mute minor hemisphere with its own very skilled performance in spatial–temporal relationships—in spatial relationships, and in music, and so on—and aesthetic judgments, etc. The left hemisphere can't even draw using the right hand. It can't even draw!

But then I would make some kind of discrimination. The left hemisphere is the speaking hemisphere, and that is the one you can talk to. I have personally met these patients and talked to them quite a bit. So that is the one that is like an ordinary human person. They can describe and have a sense of humour and talk and so on, and make their decisions for life. They've got some disabilities because of this section but not of a personal kind. With the other right hemisphere, that's the minor hemisphere so-called, you have difficulty in getting into communication. You can do it to a certain extent. There is primitive linguistic recognition, but it never can express anything in language. That is completely lost.

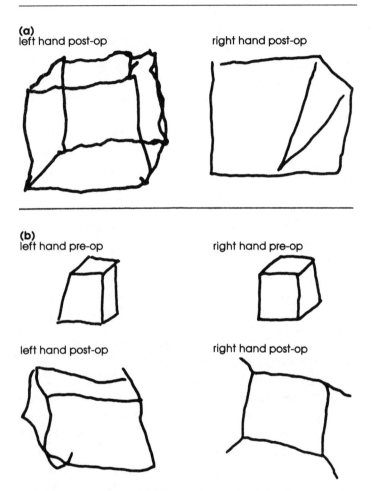

**(a)**
left hand post-op    right hand post-op

**(b)**
left hand pre-op    right hand pre-op

left hand post-op    right hand post-op

(a) The drawings made of a picture of a cube by patient WJ following the cutting of the corpus callosum in 1961. The left hand, which receives its motor control from the right (mute) hemisphere, was able to complete the task with much greater skill than the right, which receives its control from the left hemisphere which is dominant for language.

The lower section (b) shows the capacity to draw a cube with right and left hand before and after the operation. (From Michael Gazzaniga, *The Social Brain*.)

DD:   On the other hand, they do sometimes behave as if there are two people there. I remember the case Gazzaniga describes of a sinister left hand that used to proceed to undo buttons in opposition to the right— as if there were, in effect, as you were saying, two people.

JE:   Yes, that's what I'm saying too. I agree with that, but there isn't . . . the right hemisphere with this mute person. The conscious self is not, I think, a proper self in the human sense of the word, because it's not a person. It doesn't make decisions in the light of foresight, imagination, value systems and so on. This is what is missing in the performances that you get out of the right hemisphere.

DD:   With respect of aesthetics, it is capable, certainly, of initiating actions in the face of the knowledge it has—I mean of objects, and so on. In a sense it's a separate stream of consciousness . . .

JE:   Yes, but it doesn't have a proper value system in grading its actions, as far as one has been able to see from all these experiments. It is, as it were, a kind of automaton in a way, and not making subtle judgments. In the considerations, it doesn't worry about the future and the consequences of its actions. Things like that. This is what it is missing. So what I would say . . .

DD:   Are we sure that capacity is actually located? I mean, obviously, the articulation of it is in the left hemisphere in the right-handed person, but are we actually sure that it's in the left hemisphere that such judgments are embedded, as it were?

JE:   Well, Sperry is trying to say with his very advanced techniques that there is evidence that the right hemisphere does worry about the future because he puts it through all kinds of testing for whether it believes in an insurance policy and things like that, but I have not been convinced by these at all. I do not think that it knows what that insurance policy is. It has no good understanding of the subtleties of language. So by and large ...

DD:    It's not good at mathematics, is it?

JE:    No. Good at geometry, but not in arithmetic. But there is a position that I think I accept. Namely, that there are two conscious beings, you might say there, separated by the section, but not two human persons with selves in the ordinary sense of the word. Responsible, you might say ... Responsible, highly motivated human selves. The other one, it is just a performer but not a self.

DD:    Does that mean you would in effect put the soul in the left hemisphere in the right-handed person?

JE:    Yes. Well, but not, no, no, but when the corpus callosum is cut.* When it's not cut, both hemispheres are working much more together. We do not understand or allow for this nearly enough. You cut the corpus callosum, and then you think you have got two separate hemispheres, one and the other. In real life, with two to three hundred million fibres firing at one another from almost all parts of the cerebral cortex,

---

*    Retrospectively, it has occurred to me that if Sir John had sustained this view it would raise an interesting ecclesiastical problem. With many people around with split brains it is possible that sooner or later one could have a stroke which destroys the left interpretive talking cortex. Would such a person be deemed to be now without a soul, though all the appreciation of beauty and aesthetics, which is primarily a right hemisphere function, would be intact and functioning?

the cortex is one—an entity . . . And this cutting of the corpus callosum is, shall we say, a very rough treatment of this, and not one that's going to give you any subtle judgments about the functions of the left and right hemispheres.

DD:   You agreed that it shows, in a way, two separate conscious processes, as you've said. And in a way, wouldn't that—coming back to the first point that I made—wouldn't that in effect indicate that conscious-ness is an outcome of neural tissue in action, and you can have these two relatively separate neural tissues— two relatively separate, and with different capacities, streams of consciousness?

JE:   Of course, but then that is still misunderstand-ing the brain–mind problem in dualist interactionism, because what one is saying in dualist interactionism is that they are so closely locked together, the mental and the neural, interacting in a most subtle way, and with any of our tricks we can't separate them. But not that they're independent, in a sense that the initiative of action comes from the mental in all of our decision-making, in all of our ordinary human actions. It's the mental that leads the neural, but this is a very intense interaction going on. And it's not just going one way. It's backwards and forwards like that. That, I think, has not come into consideration in criticising dualism.

* * *

MEMORY AND THE SENSE OF SMELL

As we have progressed, although I've not focused on an analysis of the great issues of instinct and learning, the matter of memory has been in the interstices of

103

many discussions. It is apposite here to dwell briefly on a remarkable and fascinating aspect of the brain: that of the evolution of the sense of smell and of this faculty in humans. It has remarkable, evocative power for memory. Baudelaire in the *Flowers of Evil* writes:

And forth the ghosts of long dead odours creep—
There softly trembling in the shadows, sleep
a thousand thoughts, funeral chrysalides,
Phantoms of old the folding darkness hides.

It is patently obvious that for most of the lower mammals the areas of the brain devoted to smell predominate anatomically. It is clear from their behaviour that the acuity of this faculty far outstrips ours. The world of the animal is very much a world of smells, as demonstrated by the behaviour of our friend the dog. I suppose one of the supreme examples of the importance of smell to animals is the huge antennae of the moth. With special receptors these antennae accomplish the spectacular feat of detecting a few molecules of a scent belonging to the member of the opposite sex flying a kilometre or so upwind.

With vision and sound, the human brain has developed a stunning variety of symbolic systems to represent external events and to communicate facts and concepts. Further, a human may summon to consciousness a vision of a painting, a scene or a person and dwell upon it. Just by reading a musical score, a person may hear the music in his or her head. Most of us can summon a favourite piano concerto or any tune to mind and can play it over with remarkable accuracy. Visions and sounds are the stuff of dreams as well.

With smell, however, the matter is different. The great evolution of the front lobes of the brain, dedicated to complex mental activities of intentions, foreseeing, mathematics and images, and the temporal cortex devoted to interpretations, seems to have over-shadowed the cerebral organisation subserving smell. Lord Adrian remarked that it is uncommon for people to dream in smells. I suspect this view would be ratified by most of us. It is very uncommon for a person to lie back relaxed and be able to summon to intense conscious experience a particular odour or, for that matter, taste. The issue of whether it's possible to summon to immediate experience the odour of violets, the bouquet of a particular wine, a cheese, or a perfume—or a particular taste such as lemons—is controversial. I suspect there is a difference in being able to electively bring to consciousness the actual or specific sensation as distinct from, say, some vague sense of it. The latter could be a perceived association with the liking or disliking, together with the visual picture of yourself, say, placing your tongue on a lemon, or your nose against a rose. Be that as it may, perfume chemists and people in related businesses recognise some 30 000 different odorous chemicals, but there are only about 100 words in the English language for smell, and maybe no more than fifteen to twenty in general use. The epistemological (language) system for smell is pretty sparse. Smell has been rather buried in the brain of *Homo sapiens sapiens*.

But when we come to the matter of evocation of memory, or the setting in train of ideas in the sphere of the basic instincts such as hunger and sex, the matter is radically different. With memory, we need only turn to perhaps the most renowned passage in literature on the subject—Marcel Proust, writing in *Swann's Way* (the first volume of *Remembrance of Things Past*) about tasting *petites madeleines* decades after his early life at Combray.

Many years had elapsed during which nothing of

Combray save what was comprised in the theatre and the drama of my going to bed there had any existence for me, when one day in winter, on my return home, my mother, seeing that I was cold, offered me some tea, a thing I do not ordinarily take . . . She sent for one of those squat, plump little cakes called 'petites madeleines' which look as though they have been moulded in a fluted valve of a scallop shell . . .

And soon, mechanically, dispirited after a dreary day with the prospect of a depressing morrow, I raised to my lips a spoonful of the tea in which I had soaked a morsel of the cake. No sooner had the warm liquid mixed with the crumbs touched my palate than a shudder run through me and I stopped, intent upon the extraordinary thing that was happening to me. An exquisite pleasure had invaded my senses, something isolated, detached, with no suggestion of its origin.

I had ceased now to feel mediocre, contingent, mortal. Whence could it have come to me, this all-powerful joy? I sensed that it was connected with the taste of the tea and the cake, but that it infinitely transcended those of savours, could not, indeed, be of the same nature. Whence did it come? What did it mean? How could I seize and apprehend it? . . .

And suddenly the memory revealed itself. The taste was that of the little piece of madeleine which on Sunday mornings at Combray . . . when I went to say good morning to her in her bedroom, my Aunt Leonie used to give me, dipping it first in her own cup of tea or tisane. The sight of the little madeleine had recalled nothing to my mind before I had tasted it; perhaps because I had so often seen such things in the meantime, without tasting them, on the trays in pastry cooks' windows, that their image had dissociated itself from those Combray days . . . nothing now survived, everything was scattered, the shapes of things, including that of the little scallop shell of pastry, so richly sensual under its severe, religious folds, were either obliterated or had been so long dormant as to have lost the power of expansion which would have allowed them to resume their place in my consciousness. But when from a long distant past nothing subsists, after the people are dead, after the things are broken and scattered, taste and smell alone, more fragile but more enduring, more unsubstantial, more persistent, more faithful, remain poised a long time, like souls, remembering, waiting, hoping, amid the ruins of all the rest; and bear unflinchingly, in the tiny and almost impalpable drop of their essence, the vast structure of recollection.

But given this remarkable capacity of smells to evoke memory, there is probably a qualitative difference in the capacity to summon smells to present awareness, when compared with the agile ability to do so with music or visual art. This may not necessarily be so in the functionally deranged brain. With some forms of epilepsy, because of the site of the epileptic focus in the uncinate part of the temporal lobe devoted to smell, there may be an aura at the beginning of a fit which involves an intense sense of smelling something.

There are other neurological case reports where smell sensations may have centre stage. A startling example comes from Dr Oliver Sachs, who describes a twenty-year-old medical student who submitted his brain to cocaine, PCP, and amphetamines. One night he dreamt he was a dog and awoke to a world which was populated with smells, sharply defined in a way never before experienced. Not having had much interest in scents hitherto, he discovered that a scent shop presented an extraordinary diversity of individual odours, as did friends and patients for that matter. He felt he could smell emotions, fear, contentment, sexuality—like a dog. Indeed, his became a dog's world, and there was an immediacy to everything. He had a desire to sniff at people. And of great interest, this new quality of awareness caused thought, abstraction and categorisation—characteristic intellectual activities—to seem somewhat difficult and unreal. About three weeks later it all went away, and he returned to normal. Though glad at this, he felt some loss that these remarkable faculties had disappeared—receded, as it were, into the evolutionary night.

# 5

# Sleep and dreams

Marcel Proust wrote in *Remembrance of Things Past*:

And it was perhaps also because of the
extraordinary effects which they achieve with
time that dreams had fascinated me. Have we
not often seen in a single night, in a single
minute of a night, remote periods, relegated to
those enormous distances at which we can no
longer distinguish anything of the sentiments
which we felt in them, coming rushing upon us
with almost the speed of light as though they
were giant aeroplanes instead of the pale stars
which we had supposed them to be, blinding us
with their brilliance and bringing back to our
vision all that they had once contained for us,
giving us the emotion, the shock, the brilliance
of their immediate proximity, only, once we are
awake, to resume their positions on their far side
of the gulf which they had miraculously
traversed, so that we are tempted to
believe—wrongly however—that they are one of
the modes of rediscovering Lost Time?

I had realized before now that it is only a clumsy
and erroneous form of perception which places
everything in the object, when really everything is
in the mind.

Before encountering some of the fascinating knowledge that has accrued on the genesis of dreams, we should first look at the nature of sleep—superficially the opposite side of the coin to consciousness. In chapter 1 I mentioned the landmark observation of Constantine von Economo that the cells killed in the cases of sleeping sickness, which followed the 1918 influenza epidemic, were localised in the brain stem, and accordingly the waking condition might in fact be controlled from that area. At the time a dominant theory was that at the end of the day there was a gradual reduction of sensory inflow to the awake brain, particularly with darkness, and this reduction of inflow from the eyes and ears was a major cause of sleep. It was a theory of deprivation of sensory input. Maybe this was foreseen by Sophocles in *The Trachiniae*, where the old man says to Hyllus:

Knew I not how much better it was that
Thou shouldest keep silence, instead of
Scaring slumber from his brain and eyes

## SLEEP, AND THE EFFECT OF KNIFE CUTS ACROSS THE BRAIN STEM

An early landmark in sleep experiments was made by Dr Frederic Bremer, a Belgian neurophysiologist, in the 1930s. He found that a transverse knife cut across the top end of the brain stem of a cat caused a state of continuous drowsiness. At that time, it had also been shown by Hans Berger, a German psychiatrist, that the brain activity produced a characteristic electrical pattern, which could be recorded from the scalp. (It was called the electroencephalogram.) During sleep it was different from the awake state. Bremer's transverse cut across the upper brain stem caused the brain to have an electrical pattern characteristic of sleep in keeping with this perpetual state of torpor which came after the cut. This isolated front brain (the *cerveau isolé*) was cut off from inflow from muscles, joints, vision and sound. Smell sensation, which was untouched by the section, was the only sensation that would still activate the cat.

However, a little later on, Bremer went further. He divided the brain stem much lower down, just where the spinal cord comes through the hole at the base of the skull. To his great surprise, he found behavioural and electrical wakefulness. This preparation, called isolated fore and hind brain (*encephale isolé*), was very vigilant, although all sensory inflow from the body below the head was cut off. Thus, rather than sensory deprivation being the herald of sleep, the evidence now pointed to an active control system of arousal situated in the midbrain area between the two cuts. What had actually happened was that the first cut made higher up had interrupted the upflow from it to the grey matter of the cerebral hemispheres.

Further work by Dr Horace Magoun of Illinois, and others in America, showed that if you electrically stimulated the group of midbrain cells called the reticular activating system (or RAS) the electrical waves in these higher cortical centres changed from a big amplitude, slow wave pattern characteristic of sleep to the fast small wave of the waking state. This behavioural arousal and alertness would persist long after the electrical stimulation ceased.

## SLEEP AND AROUSAL

Thus consciousness and arousal, and sleep, are controlled from midbrain nerve cells, which integrate and

111

orchestrate the diverse and wonderful activities of the billions of cells that make up the folded grey cortical mantle of the brain hemispheres. However, the organisation is much more complex than this. There are other major components of control of sleep and arousal. In particular, a centre of nerve cells known as the suprachiasmatic nucleus in the base of the brain is a biological clock which controls the 24-hour sleep–wakefulness cycle, the circadian rhythm. Destruction of these nuclei disrupts not only sleep but many other cyclical physiological systems as well.

Estimates of the populations of cells in the human brain range up to 20 billion or higher, and because each neurone and its axons and dendrites may communicate with as many as 10 000 other neurones, there are $2 \times 10^{16}$ possible states. As Allan Hobson, of Harvard University's Department of Psychiatry, puts it in his book *The Dreaming Brain*:

> Each of the twenty billion elements generates messages at a rate varying between one hundred and two or three hundred signals per second; hence, each of the twenty billion citizens of our brain–mind is talking to at least ten thousand others at least once, and as often as one hundred times a second. With a chatterbox of such proportions it is to me just as incredible that such a system would not have awareness of itself as it is incredible that it does.

In the course of evolution it was the brain stem that was first added above the reflex mechanisms of the spinal cord. The brain stem is involved in the control of the special senses concerned with information coming from a distance—the animal's environment—eyes, ears, but also body posture. The fact that the determinant of arousal, crucial to consciousness in all higher animals, is situated in the brain stem seems to me to speak for the possibility of some rudimentary emergent conscious awareness in lower creatures, which have substantial brain stem development and analogous cellular organisation.

The electroencephalogram detects bursts of activity, cycles per second, twelve to eighteen called alpha-rhythm, when the subject is wide awake and with eyes open. When deep sleep actually comes, it develops a delta rhythm with high-amplitude slow waves at one to four cycles per second.

A crucial discovery was that during sleep there were periods when rapid eye movements occurred. Indeed, about 25 per cent of sleep time was so occupied. If you woke somebody at this particular time, it was found that they had been dreaming—that is, these periods were when dreams happened. However, some less-organised non-progressive dream states may occur in non-rapid eye movement sleep. It was also found that REM (as we will call rapid eye movement) sleep occurred in all mammals. When REM sleep and dreaming occurs in both humans and animals, the brain waves return to the fast low-amplitude type akin to the awake state, though the subject is deeply asleep. Because this seemed paradoxical to the idea of sleep, this REM sleep was dubbed by Michel Jouvet, a distinguished French pioneer in sleep research, 'paradoxical sleep'.

Now, I wonder how many readers when they dream have experienced the sensation of fear and not being able to run away or scream, and have really felt paralysed? Perhaps everybody. How come? Well, another feature of the REM sleep that was soon appreciated by the scientists as cardinal was a gross loss of tone of the muscles. In fact, this inhibition of muscle function is essential, or otherwise the subject would act out the scenario of dreams. There would be turmoil in bed. People simply could not sleep together. In fact, Jouvet has shown with cats that if he destroys the pool of neurones in the brain stem which causes this loss of muscle tone in sleep, the cat while asleep does indeed act out scenarios such as attacking imaginary prey, exploring territory, licking and washing, or showing evidence of anger. This is in no ordered sequence. It is random and haphazard, without order just like a human dream, in contrast to the behaviour of the animal when awake, when the 'pilot' is in control.

By a further sequence of experiments involving destruction of cells in the midbrain area, Jouvet showed that REM sleep was generated in the midbrain (RAS) region. It became clear that REM sleep was a characteristic of the brain of all mammals.

Eminent leaders in exploring brain function, such as Sir Charles Sherrington of Oxford, and Ivan Pavlov of St Petersburg, had believed that sleep was associated with a generalised reduction of neuronal activity in the brain. It was expected that this would be confirmed when the new techniques of electrical recording from individual cortical cells of animals were employed.

Quite the contrary was found. For example, the Nobel laureate David Hubel discovered that sensory neurones in the visual area of cats increased their rate of firing impulses when the animal went to sleep—and spectacularly so during rapid eye movement sleep. That is, the brain activates itself, and one theory is that it is rehearsing scenarios of instinctive behaviour to facilitate their function and to consolidate memory relating to them, for use in the active awake state. Such electrical activity is seen in the embryonic nervous system. It underlies the early movements of the chicken in the egg, and the human foetus kicking in the mother's womb. The electrical activity of the human foetal brain shows a sleep–wakefulness cycle with intense REM sleep. Could it be dreaming? Jean-Pierre Changeaux wonders whether the violent activity of the human foetus kicking *in utero* could resemble Jouvet's cats which had the midbrain cells destroyed. That is, the midbrain mechanisms for stopping movement and creating flacidity in sleep are not yet developed. So the movements are reflecting dreams of first movements to the mother's breast, much as the chicken's movements in the eggshell, where it opens and closes its beak, flaps wings and stretches its limbs, rehearses it for breaking the eggshell and getting out to the wide, wide world.

It is an interesting speculation. But it might be said that it is difficult to imagine how a foetus could dream. Such an idea implies images, when no external sensory information has yet been received. Otherwise it would necessitate believing that genetically programmed behaviour patterns are of sufficient complexity to generate images. This is a much larger jump than accepting that there is genetic pre-programming of the *capacity* to recognise images when they happen after birth. This latter capacity is, of course, pretty clearly shown by Dr Niko Tinbergen's beautiful demonstration of the way in which newly hatched ducks had configurational perception. If he flew a model with a short neck and long tail, just like a hawk or other bird of prey, over the baby ducks they emitted an alarm call and took cover. However, if the model were flown reversed and the long tail went first, looking like a swan rather than a hawk, they were unperturbed. They reacted instinctively to the relation of shape to movement. Indeed, as Joseph Campbell, the great scholar of mythology, remarked, even if all the hawks and similarly shaped birds became extinct, an image of their shape resides in perpetuity in the brain of the duckling or gosling. He wonders whether in our nervous system there are archaic sign stimuli, surviving from centuries of evolution during periods of the woolly mammoth and cave bear.

In any event, we know that the foetus *in utero* does receive sensory information, for this has been carefully explored in sheep by having microphones in the womb. The human foetus learns to recognise the voice of its mother. So sensory input to the child *in utero* is not ruled out.

Sleep is essential for human wellbeing. This is amply attested by the damaging effects of sleep deprivation and the real mental trauma of insomnia. The cry of humans in the early morning hours 'I've gotta get some sleep' is only too familiar. There can be a real appetite for loss of consciousness—for oblivion. As Macbeth reflects,

> Sleep that knits up the ravell'd sleave of care,
> The death of each day's life, sore labour's bath,
> Balm of hurt minds, great nature's second course,
> Chief nourisher in life's feast.

That the activity of the brain in rapid eye movement or dreaming sleep is absolutely vital has been shown, again by Jouvet. Slow wave sleep alone was not physiologically adequate for animals. Jouvet arranged for his cats to sleep on little islands surrounded by water. The cats remained awake or went into slow wave sleep, but when REM sleep began with its muscle relaxation the cats tended to slip into the water and wake up. Sustained long deprivation of paradoxical or REM sleep by this means caused aberrant behaviour, hypersexuality and eventually death. If deprived for a shorter period and then allowed to sleep the cats would, to a degree, catch up on REM sleep.

Investigations of chemicals in the brain-stem areas controlling sleep and wakefulness have advanced to the point where scientists have found different chemical transmitter systems in the pools of nerve cells subserving the functions. One type, called catecholamines, serve arousal; and another, called serotonin, serves the sleep function. More and more modern data point also to a group of peptide hormones similar to the natural opiates being involved in the fine regulation of the nerve-cell activity of the sleep system— just as researchers in other areas concerned with the instincts, such as sex, or appetites for water and minerals, have shown a veritable smorgasbord of brain hormones to be involved in the rough and fine tuning of the nerve-cell populations that govern the respective behaviours. It may be that there is a specific sleep substance produced in the brain.

There is an enormous puzzle as to what function sleep actually fulfils. Brain-imaging studies with positron emission tomography (PET), which I will explain later, show that synthesis of protein is greatest in dreamless sleep. Also, chemical mechanisms for manufacturing and supplying transmitter chemicals to the particular catecholamine cells in the midbrain which govern arousal are, in fact, fatiguable. Sleep allows them to replenish stores. These cells, as Dr Hobson of Harvard emphasises, show a consistent and dramatic decrease in firing rate during sleep, particularly REM sleep. So we also have the idea of selective resting and chemical replenishment of these particular cells, which are heavily committed to the control of attention in the waking state. Coincidentally, this process also rests the musculature of the body. But as this resting occurs in these crucial regions of the brain, other regions cut loose, as it were, and run with the ball.

The actual purpose or function of dreaming remains
a matter of debate. It is a signal feature of human
existence, because it may be calculated that in 70
years of life an individual spends about 2000 days or
six years of life in dreaming. With dreaming, the coher-
ence of consciousness and control by the will is lost,
and perception is quite dissociated from any intention
of the subject. As in *Remembrance of Things Past*:

> When a man is asleep he has in a circle around
> him the chain of the hours, the sequence of the
> years, the order of the heavenly host. Instinctively,
> when he awakes he looks to these, and in an
> instant reads off his own position in the earth
> surface, and the time which has elapsed during his
> slumbers.

I asked Dr Roger Guillemin, French-born Nobel
laureate, long-resident in the USA, whether he dreamt
in English or French, and he remarked, 'It depends
on which language is being spoken to me.'

Over the centuries, the parallel of dreams to the
waking mind of the madman or the state of halluci-
nation has been drawn. M. Moreau of Tours thought
'Madness is the dream of the waking man'. And in *A
Midsummer Night's Dream*, Theseus says to Hippolyta
and the lords:

> Lovers and madmen have such seething brains,
> Such shaping fantasies, that apprehend,
> more than cool reason ever comprehends.
> The lunatic, the lover, and the poet,
> are of imagination all compact:
> One sees more devils than vast hell can hold,
> That is, the madman; the lover, all as frantic,
> sees Helen's beauty in a brow of Egypt.

In contrast to the searchlight of attention with consciousness, there is the discordant evocation of images

in dreams. REM sleep is at its highest incidence in the foetus and very high in infancy and childhood. One body of opinion ascribes to dreaming by the developing brain the function of coupling instinct-driven propensities with new learned experience into patterns of behaviour crucial to survival functions. The content of dreams involves basic instinctive elements of feeding, fighting, escape, excretion and sex. Enacting out patterns of behaviour and rehearsing them may be of great advantage to the organism. It would have a role in the formation of circuitry in the developing brain, and thus structure. The brain is creating its own world during dreaming. The images that emerge no doubt include the repressed wishes in either obvious or disguised form (Sigmund Freud's *Royal Road to the Unconscious*), this being underlined by the characteristically sexual content of much dreaming. Penile erection and vaginal moistening occur at intervals during sleep.

While dreaming may result from the bombardment of the cortical circuits by chaotic neural volleys from the brain-stem nerve pools that orchestrate REM sleep, there is an order imposed on the results. This comes from the personality or structure of the mind of the individual dreamer. This general concept of the nature of dreaming has been termed the activation–synthesis theory by Dr Allan Hobson and his collaborator, Dr Robert McCarley, of Boston.

Francis Crick, co-discoverer with James Watson of the double helix, has in collaboration with Graeme Mitchison proposed that during waking the cortex may be overloaded with vast inflow of information. Thus REM sleep serves to erase erratic and irrelevant thoughts, which would interfere with orderly memory. Dreams are parasitic thoughts, which get expunged. However, contrary to this idea it might be noted that often one remembers dreams, and some do keep recurring. Maybe dreaming does reduce waking fantasy and obsessive thoughts. Jonathan Winston, of Rockefeller University, New York, has emphasised an evolutionary approach and pointed out that the echidna (spiny anteater) does not have REM sleep. REM emerges in mammals. However, it can be noted that there are studies of sleep in birds suggesting paradoxical sleep does occur and they have midbrain clusters of neurons similar to mammals. Winston proposes dreams to be a memory-processing mechanism where data important to survival is built into the memory bank during REM sleep.

An interesting aside of general biological interest is that Russian scientists have shown that in a sea-dwelling creature such as the dolphin there is the ability for one side only of the brain to go to sleep and show the electrical waves of REM sleep. This is obviously a brilliant adaptation to having sleep, yet keeping control of breathing in the water by the other side.

And finally, it is by no means excluded that dreams can have a creative function. The fact that solutions to problems may occur in dreaming is epitomised by Otto Loewi's renowned experience of dreaming of the experiment that won him the Nobel prize. He dreamt of stimulating the vagus nerve going to the heart of a frog which slowed its heart, and of then transferring the blood in the heart to the heart of a second animal. It proved to be the case that this slowed the heart of the second animal. This showed that a chemical substance was released when the first vagus was stimulated.

The viewpoint I am espousing here is of an increasing complexity of consciousness leading up to eventual emergence of self-awareness in the apes and humans. Consonant with this, REM sleep is universal in mam-

mals. In humans its attested function is dream generation. When taken with the clear parallel to this process in cats and dogs, not only electrophysiologically
but also behaviourally in terms of obvious dreaming
yelps in dogs, it adds a great deal more weight to
image formation in animals being a fact.

Finally in this chapter, I want to explore Dr Miriam
Rothschild's views on the role of dreams and the sense
of smell in the animal world.

DD:   In many ways smell is a quite different portal
or gateway to the psyche than other senses, and there
is a lot of evidence in relation to the human brain that
it is organised quite differently from vision and hearing, where of course there are symbolic systems developed to represent aspects of the cortical processes.
Now, with smell, it appears that, as Lord Adrian suggested, it is very uncommon for humans to dream in
smells, and on questioning people it's very unusual for
them to suggest that. Do you think when animals show
signs of dreaming they are actually dreaming in smells,
having a different sort of brain to us?

MR: Well, like so much about animals, there is a good
deal of speculation about it. But I often wonder
whether the sensation of *deja vu*, which is associated
often with smell, doesn't play a much larger part in
the lives of animals than we have thought about really,
or anticipated ourselves. It seems to me that this is a
great possibility—that an animal has this capacity of
responding to this *deja vu* sensation. I believe now that
it should be easily investigated because Professor
Richter tells me that the very cells are in the hippo-
campus. I think you can now tell exactly where the
*deja vu* sensation is produced. But I often wonder
whether that particular experience isn't associated for

animals with a great variety of smells. I think they might live in a very much more interesting world.

DD: I was wondering whether you had done any experiments when a dog has been asleep and you have actually put a smell under its nose. You've got this tremendous interest in the pyrazines. Whether you've used any odour like that, and whether it's ever been possible to evoke behaviour in the animal that is suggestive of dreaming. I mean, dogs apparently have rapid eye movement sleep, and so on, as in humans.

MR: I have never done those experiments with dogs and smell, which, of course, is something I overlooked. I haven't overlooked it, but in a way it's more difficult to do experiments with dogs and interpret them. But, of course, what I have found is that certain odours like pyrazines improve the memory—the power of recall—of animals and improve their memory not only of some specifically nasty-tasting food but of the environment in which it is found.

DD: How do they turn up naturally?

MR: The pyrazines are found in very many plants, and in very many toxic insects or toxic plants. I have come to the conclusion that they really are alerting signals which warn the animal concerned of something either nice or nasty. I mean pyrazines can appear in very delicious fruit and attract animals to that, but more often they are present in noxious insects and poisonous plants, and act as an alerting signal.

DD: Are they the same pyrazines in the two, or are they chemically different and have different odours?

MR: No. There are at least a hundred different sorts of pyrazines, but chemically slightly different—with sidechains, you know, the usual thing. The one I am working with is the same pyrazine as that which is occurring in these circumstances, and I think it is an alerting signal. It has been found now in two or three hundred insects and plants.

DD:   They are very deep-seated, aren't they? I mean, you might ask whether it is analogous to the bitter taste within the four modalities of taste. The interesting thing about bitter is, like sweet and salt, if you take a newborn baby and apply bitter substances to the tongue it immediately shows rejection reactions. It will grimace. Indeed, if you do it with an anencephalic child, that is with no cortex, you get the same response. But you get a pleasant response to sweet, indicating that these things are wired well below the cortex. Do you think the pyrazines, as alerting signals, are sort of, in a way, the analogy within the chemosenses to bitter?

MR:   Yes, sure.

DD:   Because 10 per cent of plants have got poisonous bitter-tasting alkaloids and glycosides in them, and it is a very important protective mechanism.

MR:   I think that there is a group of odours, which may really be taken as a whole, may be equivalent to bitter, but I am not sure. I mean, pyrazines are possibly very widespread, but limited. I will tell you why. Because Professor Pelosi has found in the mucosa of herbivores a pre-receptor for pyrazines. A proteinaceous receptor, a pre-receptor really for pyrazines. But it is not universal. There are some animals like goats which lack it altogether . . .

DD:   Which mucosa is this? The olfactory?

MR:   Yes, and we both feel that in the case of goats it isn't necessary to have this pyrazine receptor because it doesn't need an alerting signal. They are pretty well omnivorous and eat all the plants, whether they're poisonous or not. It seems to have an entirely different physiological mechanism for dealing with toxins. Quails among birds are slightly in the same league. They don't seem to mind these toxins much. And therefore it probably isn't as universal as bitter. I mean, I think goats might object to some bitter taste. I don't know how much they have been tested though. But certainly it is a very interesting thing to find a smell which can boost recall, and I think it might play a very important part in animal behaviour.

DD: In relation to your own view on this, can you evoke to consciousness electively a powerful sense of smell the same way as you can musical, visual things?

MR: No I can't do it, anything like a colour, for instance. I think, it is very interesting too that when you are talking about smells you can never say it's a yellow smell. You know there is no term. You have to say it's like something else.

DD: There is no language developed.

MR: There is no language for smells that I know of.

DD: Coming back to the first point—Aristotle, of course, was of the view that animals could form images and they dream. Have you any views on this? You take the view that dogs dream?

MR: Yes.

DD: In any other species, have you seen behaviour consistent with dreaming?

MR: I think that cats are a rather weaker example, but the same as dogs—I think they do show movements while they are asleep, which suggest to you that they dream, but it is not as effective.

One of the things I am now going back to is something that my foxes used to do and that cats do, which is this, I believe (I have got no proof of this), that there are many groups of human beings living in primitive communities who can't recognise pictures when they are flat, a flat photograph. They can't see the resemblance to a man. But this isn't true of foxes and cats, because when they are watching the television screen, if something occurs on that screen which is of interest they will get up from where they are sitting and go and look behind the screen to see if it's really there or not. Well, that seems to me to imply some form of thought.

DD:    It's rather analogous to the mirror situation.

MR:    Yes.

DD:    I gather that a baby in the first instance, before it becomes aware of itself, will actually look behind the mirror to see if there is something there. I gather this is also seen actually with schizophrenics looking into mirrors. They will actually look at the mirror and then look behind it in some advance cases.

The proposition has been put that man is the only animal which is aware of its future death. When an antelope or buck is being pursued by a leopard or a cheetah and is weaving and turning, do you think it has any image of its peril, impending bodily damage or annihilation? Or is it just an automaton that has registered a configuration and movement consonant with 'cheetah'? I mean, it may be genetically pre-programmed in this way and simply throws the switch on a system of evasion and weaving without any other concurrent mechanisms going on in its brain? It is

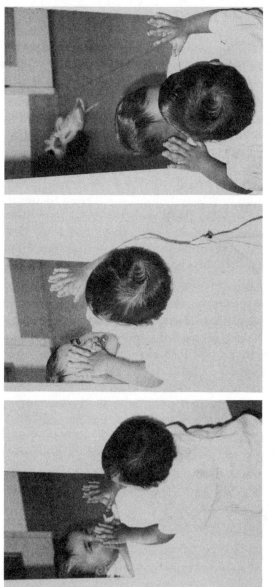

The age at which children recognise themselves in a mirror is controversial—possibly 14–20 months. Here, Benjamin, 10-month-old son of Christine Walsh, former principal ballerina with The Australian Ballet, and Ricardo Ella, on entering a dressing room sees himself in a mirror, appears delighted, and proceeds to kiss the reflection (new playmate?).

sometimes stated that buck don't automatically respond to predators that way. In fact, the prey may go over and have a look at the predator—move closer to it—and that it can, from the intentions of the predator, determine whether it's going to be attacked or not. If there is no sign of attack it will be perfectly calm, and keep an eye, as it were, on the predator, and then take evasive action when it sees some behaviour consistent with attack. I am wondering what you have seen in that area in your own experience?

MR: I confess I have never really thought very closely about it, because I have assumed that animals do not appreciate death, although they can appreciate pain and fear. They don't appreciate death, and therefore in a way I have always thought of animals as immortal because they don't know they're going to die. I remember Dr Johnson's crack about this, saying that man was immortal too, because although he knew he was going to die he never knew he was dead! I have never actually really brought my mind to bear on this question. I always remember the man, Premack, who was teaching his chimps language, and he said he never really dared go along that path because he was so afraid that if he taught these chimps real language they would appreciate death, which at that moment he was under the impression they didn't.

DD: Yes, on the present evidence, the first concrete indication of an appreciation of death comes with the Neanderthals and the ritual burial of the dead. Flowers and objects for the afterworld, and so on, came in a systematised way later. But it appears that it is only at that stage in the sequence of development of the cortex that that particular concept or appreciation emerges?

MR: There is one thing of which I have been made conscious of in animals, and that is that there is something about death which must be something to do with smell, I suppose. But there is a very generalised odour associated with death, because there is no doubt that dogs respond to a corpse in a very special way.

DD: Specifically?

MR: Yes. When the Shih tzu dog, which I mentioned earlier, was present when its co-master died—it was a joint ownership of this dog—its behaviour was very different from what it was before. It sniffed at the corpse and showed every sign of distress. That was very obvious. Now let me try and think. A doctor told me that the dogs that he knew, that he had experience with, they recognised death, and very often before he did. When the patient was dying, the dog would howl. I came to the idea that death had a special smell about it when I was doing gas chromatographs of insects. We had a bowl in which we put the insect—put a current of air through it—you know, like one could, and then analyse the air afterwards. And we found there was always a special peak appearing when an insect had died in the glass bowl. We always referred to this as a death peak—a special odour. Curiously enough, someone was experimenting in this field. I don't know if you know how often insects sham death—it's a very defensive thing.

DD: Like the freezing of certain types of rodents?

MR: Exactly. Yes. Well, they put up their legs and drop like a stone. He discovered that they imitated the smell of the dead insect (the really dead insect). They emanated an odour which resembled that. That always interested me very much. But certainly dogs seem to have some sense. Maybe it is also a sense of disaster which they feel, associated with death. I mean, other people present seem to have a special feeling in the presence of death. I have one example of that—it was very strange. My husband had a dog, a very ordinary labrador. I have written this out somewhere, this episode. He came into the room, my husband, and I had to announce to him a death that had just occurred, and before I could say anything—I was very embarrassed, I didn't know how to tell my husband this bad news—and I felt as if an iron bar was across my chest, and I couldn't speak. As I was drawing in my breath the labrador sat down, threw back its head and howled in a way that it had never made that sound before. It was like a dog howling at the moon. I looked at this animal in astonishment, and its mouth was circular as this weird howl came out. You see, the person who had died was not there in the room, so you see there couldn't have been a smell, but I think it was the feeling of disaster that the dog sensed.

DD: Jane Goodall described, of course, the way when a baby chimpanzee died, the mother carried it around for many days. What interpretation from that, whether it is grief, or some distress causes . . .

MR: Or this instinct insisting that you have to carry the young. That's impossible to say. But I certainly have never thought about whether an animal could anticipate it. But there is no doubt, to sum up what I have said, that dogs in the presence of death and the disastrous feelings that go with it experience emotional disturbance. Of that, I think, there is no doubt.

\* \* \*

# 6

# The evolution of the brain: the emergence of human society, mythology and art—the natural world engraved on consciousness

The distinguished American physician Lewis Thomas, the poet laureate of medical science, writes:

> We are, so far as we know, unique among living components of the earth for having a brain capable not only of awareness and what we call consciousness (I happen to believe that a great many other animals, including my cat and all the social insects, possess the same sort of awareness) but we do something more than this. [We record details of our past experiences and make compulsive guesses about our future. More than this, we talk to each other about these things. In short] . . . we are unique because of language. But this alone would not be enough to set us at our proper station in nature. The really important, far and away, most important thing about human beings is human society. And because of language, a literature a body of art, a feeling for music (the

strangest and thus far the best of our
achievements in my view) and when we do not in
folly suppress it, a deep appreciation for each other.

## THE GROWTH OF THE HUMAN BRAIN, THE ADVENT OF LANGUAGE

The most spectacular event in the course of evolution
has been the great increase in the size of the brain of
hominids (the humans and prehumans) during the past
three million years. Over the same period man has
emerged as the tool-maker, and the eventual extraordinary capacity of human beings to manipulate natural
forces has given a radical new turn to evolution, leading to modern civilisation. Pivotal, and no doubt generative, of this great leap forward is the emergence of
language. By emergence one does not imply, *de novo*,
on a blank canvas, but the extraordinary development
from a preliminary state involving expressions, elaborate gestures and displays. The calls and vocalisations
of our distant ancestors and those of the apes led in
time to the elaborate symbolic and abstract elements
of human language.

Of course, in the march of life from the primaeval
soup and ocean, there developed all the wondrous
processes that are embodied in the cell, with its
nucleus and genetic machinery. Then there was the
development of many-celled organisms, the metazoa,
with special tissue functions in particular organs. And
after this the emergence of the backboned creatures,
the vertebrates, with attendant bilateral symmetry.
The fish that started the march from an estuarine,
brackish-water existence and moved to land with
clumsy movements evoked the change of behaviour,
which led eventually to powerful quadruped limbs.
This Magellan of evolution, as Jacques Monod so

eloquently expresses it in his book *Chance and Necessity*, began the trail that led to the cheetahs which run at 70 to 80 kilometres per hour, the nimble creatures of the trees, and the birds that soar in the skies—as Monod theatrically states, 'amplifying the dream of the ancestral fish'.

The change in the hominids to the upright posture freed the forelimbs from commitment to walking. This gave rise to the potential of hand skills and eventually hunting. It was a great impetus to brain evolution.

Now there is no simple relation of brain weight to intelligence, as evident from the fact that the largest brains are those of elephants and whales. This reflects a relation of brain weight to body size, but it is complex in that with increasing size the proportion of body weight represented by brain decreases. This noted, it is clear that the brain of humans and, for that matter, dolphins, is large relative to body weight. This was true also of early prehumans—the australopithecenes living two to three million years ago. In the balancing of all this, we might take into account the fact that small animals to some extent achieve more computing elements than would otherwise be the case by having more of the smaller neurones, and they have them more densely packed together. Furthermore, they do not have, relatively speaking, as much supporting tissue (called the glia of the brain) per unit weight.

In humans the brain is very large, and is dominated by the cerebral hemispheres of the forebrain. It is the manner of deployment of nerve cells and their inter-relations that underlies the superior intelligence.

This change in brain size started early. *Australopithecus afarensis*, discovered in north-eastern Africa, walked upright three to four million years ago. This hominid was 120 centimetres tall and had a skull and cranial capacity of 400 cubic centimetres—about the same as that of a chimpanzee. But by two million years ago *Homo habilis* ('handy man') had begun to emerge. The brain size of 600 cubic centimetres was half as large again as the chimpanzee's. As the Leakeys established, *Homo habilis* was a tool-maker, and this is consonant with British anthropologist Kenneth Oakley's criterion of definition of true man. The tool-maker is fashioning an object for an imagined eventuality. *Homo erectus* (Java man and Peking man being representatives) emerged more than one million years ago, used ochre and fire, probably practised cannabilism, and had a brain size of about 1000 cubic centimetres. *Homo sapiens neanderthalensis* (Neanderthal man) had a brain size of about 1500 cubic centimetres and, as mentioned earlier, practised ritual burial of the dead and made fine tools. Modern *Homo sapiens sapiens* has a brain size of 1100–1500 cubic centimetres and invented art, science and civilisation.

Some time during the stages of this progression, at meteoric speed relative to the timescale of biological evolution, the capacity of symbolic expression—language—was written into the genes that dictate the organisation of the brain. That is, there is a genetic capacity for language, an inborn propensity to learn language. The developing child uses words and then goes on to develop syntax or grammar without any formal learning. This seems to occur universally over the same age span in all children and with all tongues. Apes can learn a sign language used by the deaf and string several signs together. They can even use these to cooperate for immediate needs, but it is a vast gap to the remarkable interweaving of the knowledge function and symbolic language as seen in the human child and adult. Naom Chomsky, of the Massachusetts Institute of Technology, believes there is one basic structure in all human languages, notwithstanding their diversity, and this is innate in our species. The cortex of the brain which subserves this function is being wired for it during development in the womb. In infancy and during early childhood the execution proceeds apace. The fact is that as with other developmental processes that occur in a particular time frame—I could instance the so-called critical periods at which either female or male orientation is dictated by sex hormones during brain maturation—there is a period of spontaneous acquisition of the native language. The later acquisition of a second or third language is much more difficult.

As Jacques Monod remarks, the linguistic capacity revealed in the course of the brain's unfolding of its genetic blueprint is today part of 'human nature'. And when did this begin to rapidly emerge? Well, modern neurology has clearly defined that there are two areas on one side of the brain—at the front and back of its great groove or Sylvian fissure. The front one is called Broca's area, after the French anthropologist-surgeon of the nineteenth century, and it controls the motor performance involved in speech. The rear one, Wernicke's area, in the temporal lobe, subserves the comprehension of language. With a vascular accident or stroke in Wernicke's area, the patient cannot understand words or formulate sentences, whereas with a stroke in Broca's areas, comprehension exists but the patient cannot speak.

Philip Tobias, the distinguished South African anthropologist, is of the view that the imprints made by vessels on the inner surface of the cranial cavity, which would be against the speech areas of the brain, are sufficiently evident in the skull of *Homo habilis* as to suggest that the speech area was enlarged and thus developing in this hominid more than a million years ago. Whenever it happened, it gave a survival advan-

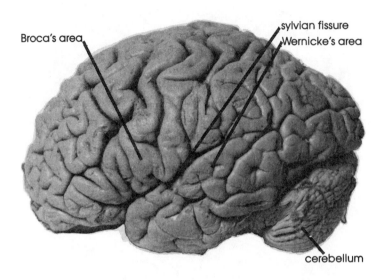

Broca's area

sylvian fissure
Wernicke's area

cerebellum

A human brain photographed to show the left hemisphere
with Broca's area (motor control of speech) and
Wernicke's area (comprehension of language) indicated.

tage, contingent on transfer of ideas, plans and information, which was immense relative to any cerebrally
comparable creature that did not have language. In
particular, with symbolism and logic the production of
mental pictures could be matched with experience of
what actually happened, and thus framing of scientific
laws finally eventuated. In a fashion, speech gave to
humans the unique advantage of Lamarkian evolution—the inheritance of acquired characteristics.
As Sir Peter Medawar said, 'In human beings, exo-
genetic heredity—the transfer of information through
non-genetic channels—has become more important for
our biological success than anything programmed in
DNA...'

135

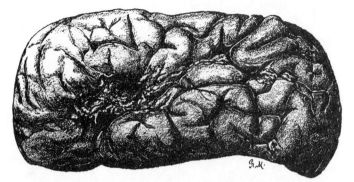

*Fig. 1.* — Hémisphère gauche du cerveau de Leborgne, première autopsie de Broca. Dessin fait sur la photographie de la pièce actuellement conservée au Musée Dupuytren. On voit que, en outre de la lésion de la troisième frontale, le ramollissement existait tout le long de la scissure de Sylvius et siégeait par conséquent aussi dans la zone de Wernicke.

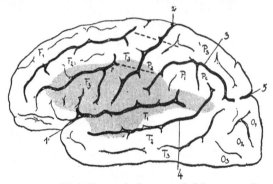

*Fig. 2.* — Hémisphère gauche du cerveau de Leborgne, première autopsie de Broca; traduction, en schéma, des lésions que l'on constate sur la pièce conservée au Musée Dupuytren. — (Comparer avec le dessin de la pièce elle-même, *fig. 1.* — La grande rétraction subie par les circonvolutions est la cause de la discordance qui, au premier abord, semble exister entre ces deux figures.) La plus grande partie du territoire Sylvien, y compris la zone de Wernicke, est atteinte.

An illustration of the brain of Broca's patient Leborgne showing (*top*) the destruction at the lower part of the left frontal lobe which extended back along the superior part of the temporal lobe. The lower diagram shows the extent of the softening. The patient's only words were 'tan-tan'. The observation was pivotal in showing that behaviour could be linked to a particular cerebral location.

## CULTURAL INFLUENCES ACCELERATING BRAIN DEVELOPMENT

To help in finding an explanation of the enormous acceleration of brain development (including language) in the hominids, Edward Wilson of Harvard and Charles Lumsden of Canada have proposed a basis in gene–culture co-evolution, which is seen as an autocatalytic or a self-propelling process with tight linkage between genetic evolution and cultural history. They say, in orthodox terms, that evolution in insects and small-brained animals occurs when mutation, or recombination of existing genes, gives a novel behaviour. If this novelty bestows higher survival or success in reproduction, the genes prescribing it will spread in the population.

Human evolution is both similar and profoundly different. Culture can transform heredity. New forms of behaviour, leaps of culture, can be invented by the mind. However, which forms occur are greatly influenced by the genes. These determine which stimuli are perceived, which missed, which information is processed, which emotions are most likely to be aroused, and so on. These so-called epigenetic rules are rooted in the human biology. But, and this is the crucial point, the mind, as culture, intervenes decisively. It permits each combination of genes to have multiple expressions and offers alternative solutions to many problems, even within a lifetime. Great or spectacular biological success of a particular behaviour may cause dominance of the individual or individuals in a group, and as a result they get more mates so a reproductive success follows. Thus the gene combination subserving some behavioural success spreads through the population. Future generations are more likely to develop the behaviour and thought underlying it. Thus the culture has changed the direction of genetic evolution and greatly accelerated it.

Culture is a rapid-acting force for change, and obviously in a small group a single exceptional, extremely gifted individual, with both aggression and cooperation skills, can have a profound effect on the future direction—just as elimination of such an individual or small group can point a community to decline or even extinction. What circumstances might have done this? Well, Darwin recognised that a new art in conduct of intertribal warfare could have been such a powerful selective force. The innate qualities of the victors spread through the conquered, as a result of an acquisition of territory and abundant new mating options. Lumsden and Wilson hypothesise that in 1000 years or fifty generations substantial genetic evolution in the innate rules governing thought and behaviour could occur. They instance, as an illustration, the possibility that one gene characterising facial expression of displeasure could be selected for in a small population, and in successive generations over the period of one or a few thousand years, could displace the influence of another determining, say, flaring of the nostrils as the flag of psychological status.

In the course of discussions with Sir John Eccles, in relation to the argument outlined above, I cited the discovery of fire, which turned part of the night into day. It would be an example of a cultural change with the potential of enormous irradiating effect. It could nurture many consequent social and cultural patterns bestowing high survival advantage. In a real way the discovery of elective use of domestic fire, with its sociological consequences, could constitute some parallel or analogy of the hypothesis of 'punctuated equilibria' of Drs Niles Eldredge and Stephen Jay Gould of Harvard University, whereby in evolution new species or, in this case, at least new ethnic groups emerged—that is, a small population, peripheral or otherwise to a main group, which started using fire could have achieved a spectacular advance in their life in caves. For them it extended the hours the group were awake. This stimulated the development of language, particularly in order to frame strategies for more successful hunting. It provided heat for the fashioning of materials. It greatly extended nutritional options because cooking made the inedible digestible, destroyed plant poisons and, in the case of scavenged meat, destroyed micro-organisms and thus reduced gastrointestinal setbacks. Furthermore, apart from use in caves, fire at night for hunting groups on the savanna may have protected them from predatory carnivores. Overall it could have given an increased dominance to leaders who initiated it. This could increase the numbers of the group with prevalence of their particular genetic organisation, so that a new and quite different ethnic or cultural group might arise—a parallel in some respects to the development of new species in animal populations. Further to this, as Curt Richter of Johns Hopkins University noted, the emancipation from the constant twelve-hour day/twelve-hour night cycle of the tropics may well have set the stage for the migration to a European habitat, where there is large seasonal variation in hours of light and dark, and being asleep for six hours of the long summer day could be dangerous.

As well as language, social organisation is held by Nicholas Humphrey to have been a cardinal influence on brain evolution. Field observation of gorillas in Africa greatly influenced him. The gorillas apparently had a tranquil existence in family groups led by one or two males. They tended not to get up from their nests too early in the morning, they fed on vine shoots or wild celery, they napped and did not range more than a kilometre or two in the afternoon to a new camp site. Mainly they eat, rest and play, and seemingly life is rather easy, though the gorilla has a large brain—presumptively, much larger than needed for the easy life. On pondering the problem, in the face of evident intelligence of gorillas when in a laboratory setting and given tests, Humphrey concluded that gorilla society is stable because they are accomplished at making it so. There are small skirmishes, tests of dominance in relation to different goals of food access, grooming and nest sites, and sometimes more serious and very dangerous conflict. Then this is a matter of life and death with brutal fights between silverbacks, the leading males. So it is not in the environment but in the behaviour of other gorillas wherein danger lies. Thus it is postulated that gorillas need every bit of intelligence to handle this. They need to be natural psychologists and deeply sensitive to the responses of their fellows to situations.

The parallel extends naturally to early hominid societies and maybe to modern parallels such as the Kalahari bushmen, whose lifestyle in many respects may not have changed a great deal over hundreds of thousands of years. There are the divisions of labour between sexes in a hunter–gatherer society. The formalities of sexual relations, child-rearing and the hierarchical tribal structure with dominance are all set among some measure of petty jealousies, infidelities, domestic feuds and squabbles, which require constant exercise of psychological skills to prevent violence and social fragmentation. With contemporaneous increase of language facility, the question of what people said to each other and thought, along with the eventual development of myths concerned with formalising their behaviour patterns in the light of beliefs, all contributed to cerebral evolution. Dawning insight of how to contrive and stage-manage cooperative activities must have carried a big premium. Above all, it could have accelerated self-awareness—already present in the social chimpanzee, as we have recounted—so there was the inward turning of consciousness and scrutinising one's own reactions.

The validity of these anthropological scenarios of the pressures to acute observation and prediction of behaviour of fellows is transparently obvious within the ambit of experience of almost any participant in modern-day business, academic or political committees, or discussion meeting. Let there be an individual who is aggressive, bullying and placed in the position of power and dominance, and most members of a committee have eyes fixed on the aforesaid, rather than the speaker of the moment, to see if the speaker's words cause a cloud to cross the sun of the visage. One can imagine that it would have been much like this at a Politburo meeting with Stalin in the seat.

## THE AWARENESS OF THE TRANSIENCE OF EXISTENCE AND DEATH

I would now like to address three of the multitude of facets of the conscious function of the human brain: the awareness of eventual death, the emergence of the exhilaration imparted to the psyche by the natural world, and the emergence of artistic expression. Self-evidently and transparently so, they are much more than purely scientific questions. At least, the latter two are, although questions as to origins have scientific elements. But just as Pope Paul VI at the Pontifical Academy conference on brain and conscious experience defined his view and offered help in the matters of which he proposed the Church was trustee, 'whenever the learned researchers bring you to the threshold to those grave questions which transcend the domain of science', in like vein, it can be recognised that many people in the arts do not wholly welcome the intrusion of any inquiry by the scientific mind, particularly if it is of reductionist bent, into any segment of their holy grail.

Notwithstanding, it seems intriguing to question and speculate about the seeds or origins in early human society of expressions, thoughts and capacities that have flowered exuberantly in the creative arts of our world today. Of course, it is just this curiosity which is the engine driving the pursuit of anthropology and archaeology.

The flower tributes first seen with the burial of Neanderthal dead 70 000 to 90 000 years ago perhaps reflect the first emergence of myths and religion, and the sadness at the transitory nature of life and existence of the self. Certainly a new emergent in awareness is implicit—perhaps embodied millennia later in Prospero's words in *The Tempest*, by William Shakespeare:

Our revels now are ended. These our actors,
As I foretold you, were all spirits and
Are melted into air, into thin air:
And, like the baseless fabric of this vision,
The cloud-capp'd towers, the gorgeous palaces,
The solemn temples, the great globe itself,
Yea, all which it inherit, shall dissolve
And, like this insubstantial pageant faded,
Leave not a rack behind. We are such stuff
As dreams are made on, and our little life
Is rounded with a sleep.

It is evocative to reflect on a few of the innumerable

ways this inexorable finality of death has been seen in different cultures. Of this Achilles says in *The Iliad*:

> But man's life will come not again, nor will it be captured.
> Once it has passed through his teeth, nor can
>    any power restore it.

The ghost of the mother of Odysseus tells him:

> This is the law of mortals; whenever anyone dieth
> Then no longer are bones and flesh held
>    together by sinews.
> But by the might of the blazing fire they are
>    conquered and wasted.
> From that moment when first the breath departs
>    from the white bones
> Flutters the spirit away, and like to a dream it
>    goes drifting.

Perhaps Gauguin's sense of approaching evensong of his existence is seen in his painting of the Tahitian interior with the wilting sunflowers, while beyond the window two young Tahitians gambol in the water beside a pirogue.

Proust had, perhaps, a more sardonic view:

> To me it seems more correct to say that the cruel law of art is that people die and we ourselves die after exhausting every form of suffering, so that over our heads may grow the grass not of oblivion but of eternal life, the vigorous and luxuriant growth of a true work of art, and so that thither, gaily and without a thought for those that are sleeping beneath them, future generations may come to enjoy their lunch on the grass.

There are many accounts of moping and pining in social and pair-bonded animals following the death of one, and similarly between pet and master.

143

Chimpanzee mothers may carry around their dead infant for a long time. Such observations are very difficult to interpret, particularly with the paucity of evidence bearing on anticipation of impending death by animals.

There is one carefully documented account of an accidental violent death in a chimpanzee troupe in the Gombe Stream. Geza Teleki recounts how the whole troop witnessed Rix fall, and a boulder snapped his neck. The males began complex displays with hair erect, swaggering on two legs, slapping and stamping the ground, tearing vegetation and throwing stones. Most of the group were shrieking with eerie 'wraah' calls echoing. Each chimpanzee was seen to stop and stare at the motionless corpse, start calling, and pat and embrace one another. One threw stones at the corpse, while three others sat a short distance from the body, staring but not prepared to touch it. Teleki writes:

> Hugo then steps closer still, stands right next to the body, and peers down at it for several minutes; he then launches into a vigorous display away from the corpse. Hugo and Mike also charge away in different directions, ripping down vegetation as they run. Meanwhile, Godi and Sniff have been steadily wraahing while staring fixedly at the body from a distance of several meters; others join in the calling more sporadically. The three males return from their displays, soon followed by others, and at least twelve individuals now gather round the body, forming a rough circle of about 5–8 metres diameter; all but Godi, who wraahs steadily, sit in silence and gaze at Rix.

The distress of the chimpanzees lasted for more than three hours, when the top-ranking chimpanzee led the troop away, although all seemed reluctant to be parted from their dead companion. All peered over their shoulders until the body of Rix was out of sight. The event raised in Teleki's mind the issue of the role of cognitive processes in an event of death in a chimpanzee troop, whether in the face of the agonised behaviour there was a grasp of the conceptual difference between life and death, and whether, in fact, recognition of significance of death long preceded Neanderthal ritual burial—given the chimpanzees' self-concept powers. Jane Goodall has described how the young chimpanzee Flint, who was particularly attached to his old mother, Flo, stayed close to her body for six days after she died, and showed increasing signs of lethargy. His physical condition deteriorated and he died about three weeks later.

This issue remains a matter of conjecture. Maybe the experiments I recounted in chapter 3, on despair in wild rats, indicate the beginnings of some dim awareness. Adding to the evidence of bonding in animals, Professor W.H. Thorpe, the great zoologist of Cambridge University, recounts an extraordinary friendship described for two male bottle-nosed dolphins. Though long-time rivals for the attentions of a female who was sexually receptive at that time, when reunited after some weeks apart the two recognised each other and swam side by side frenziedly through the water. For days they were inseparable and paid no attention to the female.


THE IMPACT OF NATURE ON THE MIND: PANTHEISM


The idea of human consciousness as an emergent, as life progressed from the primaeval brine to its present heights, seems intrinsically compatible and indeed generative of the sense that consciousness embodies an overwhelming sense of oneness with nature. From this arises a deep joy in the forests, the oceans, the light of the stars, and the beauty of animals. Of course, the sheer power of natural forces also inspired fear and awe. But the sensory inflow from the natural world engraves one particular character to consciousness, an aesthetic element. And, of course, there is manifest in literature, poetry and art a deep love of the physical world.

Apart from the expression of this powerful emotion in art, its strength to determine behaviour of twentieth-century humans is obvious in the driving determination of the 'Greens' and the conservation movement worldwide. It has become a powerful political force fervently committed to defending the shrinking wilderness. E.O. Wilson has said of cutting down the Amazon rainforest that 'The action can be defended with difficulty on economic grounds, but it is like burning a Renaissance painting to cook dinner.' Parenthetically, I remember that about the first science fiction I read had the space voyager, after a long time away, returning to 'the cool green fields of Earth'.

Probably the most eloquent and compelling contemporary scientific proposal of mankind's oneness with nature is the Gaia hypothesis of British chemist James Lovelock and microbiologist Lynn Margulis. The name derives from Gaia, the Greek goddess of the earth, reflecting its origin in an ancient myth. In essence it regards the planet itself as a single living organism with inextricably interdependent parts, the life processes themselves being as determinant of the environment in which they flourish as the converse. All living matter of the planet, together with the oceans, the diverse rocks of the earth and the oxygen-rich atmosphere, is a complex self-organising system wherein a vast variety of processes contrive the existing planetary environment.

But it can be asked whether or not the sense of joy in the natural world is an intrinsic inborn part of the human constitution? Is it genetically programmed as a physiological elation, which can come from some fusion of sensory inflow from the eyes, the sounds of the wild, the touch of the wind on the skin—there being inherent propensities for delight in these things, which reside ultimately in the fact that the nervous system has evolved in a fashion such that these inflows can give an exuberant sense of physical wellbeing. That is, exhilaration is a physiological reality and requires physiological explanation by way of mechanisms in the brain.

Viscount Grey of Falladon wrote in relation to the joys of *Fly Fishing*:

> ... After a few days of exercise in the air of the North, there come times when the angler, who wanders alone after sea trout down glens and over moors, has a sense of physical energy and strength beyond all his experience in ordinary life. Often after walking a mile or two on the way to the river, at a brisk pace, there comes upon one a feeling of 'fitness', of being made of nothing but health and strength so perfect, that life need have no other end but to enjoy them ... The pure act of breathing at such times seems glorious. People talk of being a child of nature, and moments such as these are the times when it is possible to feel so; to know the full joy of animal life—to desire nothing beyond. There are times when I have stood still for joy of it all, on my way through the wild freedom of a Highland moor, and felt the wind, and looked upon the mountains and water and light and sky, till I felt conscious only of the strength of a mighty current of life, which swept

away all consciousness of self, and made me a part
of all that I beheld.

I suppose as an alternative it is necessary to ask: Are
these reactions culturally acquired? And perhaps, as
such, are they a counterbalance to our civilisation, with
its technology and sometimes sterile uniformity? That
is, have we needed, and found, an antidote to it all in
retreat to the natural world? However, gainsaying this,
there is no doubt that the expression of joy in nature
in art antecedes by millennia the technological world,
and for the poets the intuition that the sense is intrinsic to our being is pre-eminent.

The exhilaration in nature changes in the individual
with growth and diversification of knowledge, and this
maturation of the mind was beautifully expressed by
Wordsworth in the lines written above Tintern Abbey,
when he said of the sylvan River Wye, 'thou wanderer
through the woods'.

> When first I came among these hills; when like a
>     roe
> I bounded o'er the mountains, by the sides
> Of the deep rivers, and the lonely streams,
> Wherever nature led—more like a man
> Flying from something that he dreads than one
> Who sought the thing he loved. For nature
>     then . . .
> To me was all in all—I cannot paint—
> What then I was. The sounding cataract
> Haunted me like a passion; the tall rock,
> The mountain, and the deep and gloomy wood,
> Their colours and their forms, were then to me
>     an appetite.

But he reflects as he grew older:

For I have learned to look on nature, not as in

the hour
Of thoughtless youth; but hearing oftentimes
The still, sad music of humanity,
Nor harsh nor grating, though of ample power
To chasten and subdue. And I have felt
A presence that disturbs me with the joy
Of elevated thoughts; a sense sublime
Of something far more deeply interfused,
Whose dwelling is the light of setting suns,
And the round ocean, and the living air,
And the blue sky, and in the mind of man.

Elements of this joy of youth and its emotions expressed by Wordsworth are perhaps not entirely removed from the play of animals, akin to the young foals galloping around the pasture with no evident goal except, perhaps, the sheer pleasure of it. However, as with the play of cubs, kittens and other young, there is in this a vital biological role in rehearsing elements of instinctive programs that are crucial to subsequent success of the creature in hunting, evasion and the struggle for survival. Rehearsal of stalking and pouncing which is repeated may give an intrinsic satisfaction by virtue of the animal's own perception and sense of executing a repertoire. With the successful execution of motor elements of play and enactment of future scenarios vital to existence there is an excitement that gives release of hormones which affect heart, brain and skin, and these humours thus released initiate their own class of sensation from these organs to feed back to the general sense of exhilaration. The sense may even be served by associated release in localised areas of the brain of its own natural opiates, the endorphins and enkephalins.

However, the jump is enormous from the exuberance of the young bounding in the natural world to mankind's sense of awe at the vastness of the cosmos.

A painting of a horse on the wall of a cave at Lascaux in the Dordogne, France.

The wonder at the heavens is intrinsically contemplative, not active, and is coupled to the ever-growing human knowledge of the physical dimensions underlying what is contemplated. But again, the sense of beauty and delight in the heavens anteceded the knowledge of the immensity of the universe, which grew rapidly from the time of the Renaissance.

If one is to sustain the view that there can be some conscious states ranging from pleasure to ecstasy engendered by the sensory inflow from the natural world, there are other basic questions to be addressed. If it be so, what are the behavourial manifestations, individual and collective, which would suggest some generality of the phenomenon in *Homo sapiens sapiens*? This is distinct from such an idea being a romantic invention of any particular society or ethnic isolate. One first answer must reside in the universality of art in human society—beginning, of course, with the prehistoric art of Cro-Magnon man. This behaviour—the desire and need to depict and create in order to reflect what is seen and felt as beautiful and inspiring—as well as serving other pragmatic purposes, testifies to the generality. From Aurignacian Cro-Magnon art in the caves of the Dordogne and Bordeaux (about 35 000 years ago), the Khmer, the Tang, the Greek, the Asmat in New Guinea, the Renaissance in Florence, Turner in Britain, and the Australian Aborigines, these and innumerable other instances show the universal delight in the beauty of animals, nature, and humans over the millennia. Cezanne said: 'Art is a harmony parallel to nature.'

The great scholar of mythology and anthropology, Joseph Campbell, quotes the chief of the American Indian Pawnee Tribe, Letakots-Lesa:

> In the beginning of all things, wisdom and knowledge were with the animals; for Tirawa, the One Above, did not speak directly to man. He sent certain animals to tell man that he showed himself through the beasts, and that from them, and from the stars and the sun and the moon, man should learn. Tirawa spoke to man through his works.

Campbell suggests that the prime role of mythology is to awaken in the individual the sense of wonder and awe and participation in the inscrutable universe, as the artist, the modern physicist, and leaders of Oriental religions have done. The sense of the imminent, the tremendous mystery and fascination, gives basis to the sense of self.

He sees a great impact of nature on mythology and art. The impact is reflected by the difference between that mythology of the great Plains dwellers of postglacial Europe, Siberia and North America, and those of the tropical equatorial jungle belt where plants, not animals, have been the chief source of sustenance; and women, not men, the dominant providers.

The landscape of the Great Hunt was a spreading plain bounded by a circular horizon, with a blue dome of an exalted heaven above, hovering eagles and blazing sun and, with night, the blaze of stars and the waxing and waning moon. Dangerous encounters with grazing herds and the sense of a covenant with the animals gave rise to various rituals in which life blood of animals was given back to the all-sustaining earth.

At the opposite extreme, the environment of a dense and mighty foliage of a jungle ... with a canopy of prodigious trees, shrieking birds, no dome of sky, and underfoot a dangerous leaf mat in which lurked fangs and stings, carried the lesson that from out of death springs life and new birth, and indeed to increase life the way is to increase death. The entire equatorial belt—Africa, Asia, Oceania and Middle America and Brazil—embodies rituals of sacrifice, vegetable, animal and human, and these rituals have survived in myths and communions.

Campbell goes on to say that it has always been the business of the great seers, prophets, shamans or, today, the poets and artists, to embody the function of mythology 'by recognizing through the veil of nature, as viewed in the science of their times, the radiance, terrible yet gentle of the dark unspeakable light beyond'.

## AESTHETICS AND ANIMALS

Given our evolutionary overview, the question may be asked as to whether there is evidence of aesthetic appreciation exhibited by animals. It is hard to prove, but Professor Thorpe, who perhaps thought as much about this as anyone, proposed there are plausible reasons for supposing there are glimmerings of it. The male bowerbirds of Australia establish display grounds to attract females, though the nests are built away from the bowers. The bowers are decorated in elaborate ways with objects including brightly coloured flowers and fruits, not to be eaten, but which are changed by the bird when they wither. Others paint the walls of the bower with fruit pulp, or use a painting tool made out of a small wad of absorbent bark. Some species not only select objects that seem beautiful to humans but also vigorously maintain a colour scheme so that a bird using blue flowers and colours will remove a yellow flower inserted by the watcher, or vice versa. Thorpe suggested it seems impossible to deny that a well-adorned bower may give the bird a pleasure which can only be called aesthetic. He thinks also that the critical investigation of songs of some species of birds shows evidence of spontaneous rearrangement of phrases and emergence of novel material, suggesting something akin to real musical invention. Peter Marler, an early colleague of Donald Griffin at Rockefeller University, emphasises this improvisation on a memorised theme, exchange between songs and outright invention. Fernando Nottebohm of the Rockefeller University, who has studied song production by birds, finds each side of the bird's brain has pathways for song production and learning. In some species, such as the catbird, each side produces a unique set of sounds, although the amount produced by each side is about balanced. In the canary the left half of the brain contributes a majority of sound syllables. Szoke has argued that inasmuch as humans use intervals of the natural series of overtones, these must have been learned from the environment, as they are not necessitated by the nature of our vocal equipment. It thus seems possible

Spotted bowerbird (*Photo*: Graham Pizzey)

that the intervals acceptable to the human ear as normal and natural for music are, in fact, the intervals that were first offered to the ancestors of man by birdsongs. Birds were all around, and palaeolithic man had the palaeomelody of the birds. Thorpe also thinks that in early dancing, the headdresses and displays may have mimicked the birds. He raises the question as to why the display plumes of many birds and of butterflies produced by evolution as recognition patterns for sexual behaviour appear as very beautiful to us. In particular, he stresses that some singing of birds is independent of territorial marking or the breeding cycle and appears to represent experiment with sound. This is seen particularly with some American songbirds and the skylark in Europe.

NATURE AND ART

In further contemplating that art and literature may

often take their form and structure from what is inherent in our relation to nature, I wish to turn to the expression of feelings by several great writers at the time they gave their Nobel orations. Saul Bellow described his great debt to Joseph Conrad in awakening him. Conrad, he says, felt that

> ... art was an attempt to render the highest justice to the visible universe. That it tried to find in that universe in matter as well as in the facts of life, what was fundamental enduring, essential. Conrad felt that the method of attaining the essential was different from the thinker or scientist. The artist had only himself. He descended within himself and in the lonely regions to which he descended he found the terms of his appeal.

The appeal, Conrad said, was

> to that part of our being which is a gift, not an acquisition, to the capacity for delight and wonder ... our sense of pity and pain, to the latent feeling of fellowship with all creation.

The great Chilean poet Pablo Neruda described how he had to cross the Andes to find the border of his own country and Argentina and his liberty—a journey he made with four companions. It was a journey on horseback without tracks or paths. He recounts how each of them made his way forward filled with this limitless solitude, with the green and white silence of trees and huge trailing plants and layers of soil laid down over centuries, among half-fallen tree trunks which suddenly appeared as fresh obstacles to bar their progress:

> During this long journey I found the necessary components for the making of the poem. There is received contributions from the earth and from the

soul. And I believe that poetry is an action, ephemeral or solemn, in which there enter as equal partners, solitude and solidarity, emotion and action, the nearness to oneself, the nearness to mankind and to the secret manifestations of nature ... We are conscious of our duty as fulfillers and we feel also the responsibility for reawakening the old dreams which sleep in statues of stone in the ruined ancient monuments, in the wide-stretching silence in planetary plains, in dense primeval forests, in rivers which roar like thunder. We must fill with words the most distant places in a dumb continent.

Yasunari Kawabata speaks eloquently of the deep influence of nature on Japanese poetry. He quotes the priest Myoe (1173–1232):

> The winter moon comes from the clouds
>   to keep me company
> The wind is piercing, and snow is cold.

and

> Opening my eyes from my meditations, I saw
> the moon in the dawn, lighting the window.
> In a dark place myself, I felt as if my own heart
> were glowing with light which seemed to be that
> of the moon.

The priest Ikkyu (1394–1481), a mediaeval calligraphist, wrote:

> And what is it, the heart?
> It is the sound of the pine breeze in the ink
>   painting.

A benefit of having lived many summers is that some readers will have seen Greece and Athens before the change of the recent twenty years. To be able to go by yourself to the Parthenon at night and see the moonlight on the Aegean while standing between the towering Doric columns, or climb into the stadium at Delphi with the dawn, or to seek out Ictinos' other masterpiece, the Temple at Bassae in the Peloponnese at dawn, was to etch Greece deep on the memory.

Sir Maurice Bowra, of Oxford University, sees this impact of nature as a prime force on the Greek eye and shaping the mind. He speaks of the commanding beauty of the land which forces itself slowly and unforgettably on the traveller:

What matters above all is the quality of the light. Not only on the cloudless days of summer, but in the winter the light is different to any other European country. It sharpens the edges of the mountains against the sky ... It gives an ever-changing design to the folds and hollows as the shadows shift on and off them; it turns the sea to opal at dawn, to sapphire at midday, and in succession to gold, silver and lead before nightfall; it outlines the dark green of the olive trees in contrast to the rusty or ochre soil ... The beauty of the Greek landscape depends primarily on the light and thus had a powerful influence on the Greek vision of the world.

Just because by its very strength and sharpness the light forbids the shifting, melting, diaphanous effects which give so delicate a charm to the French or Italian scene.

Bowra felt the Greek light stimulates a vision that belongs to the sculptor more than the painter, depending on a clearness of outline, a sense of mass, of bodies emphatically placed in space, of strength and solidity behind natural curves and protuberances. Such a landscape and such a light impose their secret discipline on the eye and make it see things in contour and relief

... They explain why the Greeks produced great sculptors and architects.

Bowra proposes also that it is not fanciful to think the Greek light helped form Greek thought—influencing the clearcut conceptions of Greek philosophy—a consistent straightforward vocabulary for abstract ideas, in contrast to the cloudy skies of northern Europe giving the amorphous progeny of Norse mythology or German metaphysics.

Andre Malraux, the distinguished French savant, reflects that whilst our civilisation is the most powerful the world has ever known it is cut off from the cosmos.

> Greek civilisation is inseparable from the fact that it is linked to the cosmos by its gods. Any Greek god you care to name is a mediator between the cosmos and man via a specific group of natural forces ... The Middle Ages experienced this continuity in a completely different way but still very strongly. God made the evening and the morning and good Christian folk were linked to their God by the bells that rang them in. The Angelus was a time of day but it was also the Angel of Annunciation.

The exuberant delight in nature as a dominant element of consciousness is as much the province of the experimental biologist as the poet. Or, hopefully, many biologists are poets and, as such, not very well disguised.

E.O. Wilson says in his book *Biophilia*:

> And now to the heart of wonder. Because species diversity was created prior to humanity and because we evolved within it we have never fathomed its limits. As a consequence the living world is the natural domain of the most restless and paradoxical part of the human spirit. Our sense of wonder grows exponentially, the greater

the knowledge the deeper the mystery, and the more we seek knowledge to create new mystery.

He reflects on the human affinity for other forms of life, and that we are endlessly fascinated by plants and animals and weave them into our art, mythology and religion.

To me an eloquent and simple testimony of human need and hunger for the verdant and flowers is the sight one has on driving from Hong Kong airport along Wanchi to central Hong Kong. Literally thousands of balconies on the concrete ant heap are festooned with countless pot plants and flowers.

Wilson thinks that to explore and affiliate with the other living creatures of the planet is a deep and complicated process in mental development. He reflects that most species of organisms have genetic codes as complex as that of human beings and histories millions of years older. We are literally immersed in the traces of the deep history that produced us. Jacques Monod touches the heart of this when he says: 'Every living being is also a fossil.'

# 7

# Thinking and the events in the brain

## LOWER ANIMALS AND THOUGHT

Earlier in this book, discussion with Dr Donald Griffin touched upon the issue of whether in the behaviour of bees, particularly swarming, there was any indication of some nascent awareness in creatures relatively low in the scale of life. An episode recounted by Nobel laureate Konrad Lorenz in his delightful book on animal behaviour *King Solomon's Ring* is, to say the least, provocative on this question. In this instance it concerns jewel fish, and the father and mother putting their babies to bed at night. The mother, Lorenz says,

> jerks her fin rapidly up and down, making the jewels flash like a heliograph. At this, the young congregate under the mother and obediently descend into the nesting hole. The father, in the meantime searches the whole tank for stragglers. He does not coax them along but simply inhales them into his roomy mouth, swims to the nest, and blows them into the hollow. The baby sinks at

160

once heavily to the bottom and remains lying
there. By an ingenious arrangement of reflexes,
the swim-bladders of young 'sleeping' cichlids
contract so strongly that the tiny fishes become
much heavier than water and remain, like little
stones, lying in the hollow, just as they did in their
earliest childhood before their swim-bladder was
filled with gas. The same reaction of 'becoming
heavy' is also elicited when a parent fish takes a
young one in its mouth. Without this reflex
mechanism it would be impossible for the father,
when he gathers up his children in the evening, to
keep them together.

I once saw a jewel fish, during such an evening
transport of strayed children, perform a deed
which absolutely astonished me. I came, late one
evening, into the laboratory. It was already dusk
and I wished hurriedly to feed a few fishes which
had not received anything to eat that day; amongst
them was a pair of jewel fishes who were tending
their young. As I approached the container, I saw
that most of the young were already in the nesting
hollow over which the mother was hovering. She
refused to come for the food when I threw pieces
of earthworm into the tank. The father, however,
who, in great excitement, was dashing backwards
and forwards searching for truants, allowed himself
to be diverted from his duty by a nice hind-end of
earthworm (for some unknown reason this end is
preferred by all worm eaters to the front one). He
swam up and seized the worm, but, owing to its
size, was unable to swallow it. As he was in the act
of chewing this mouthful, he saw a baby fish
swimming by itself across the tank; he started as
though stung, raced after the baby and took it into
his already filled mouth. It was a thrilling moment.
The fish had in its mouth two different things of
which one must go into the stomach and the other
into the nest. What would he do? I must confess

that, at that moment, I would not have given twopence for the life of that tiny jewel fish. But wonderful what really happened! The fish stood stock still with full cheeks, but did not chew. If ever I have seen a fish think, it was in that moment! What a truly remarkable thing that a fish can find itself in a genuine conflicting situation and, in this case, behave exactly as a human being would; that is to say, it stops, blocked in all directions, and can go neither forward nor backward. For many seconds the father jewel fish stood riveted and one could almost see how his feelings were working. Then he solved the conflict in a way for which one was bound to feel admiration: he spat out the whole contents of his mouth: the worm fell to the bottom, and the little jewel fish, becoming heavy in the way described above, did the same. Then the father turned resolutely to the worm and ate it up, without haste but all the time with one eye on the child which 'obediently' lay on the bottom beneath him. When he had finished, he inhaled the baby and carried it home to its mother.

Some students, who had witnessed the whole scene, started as one man to applaud.

The story rather highlights the question of status of anecdote that I discussed in the Introduction. Given the high probability that Dr Lorenz observed and recorded accurately the exact sequence of events, as perhaps ratified by the students present, the puzzle centres on the collision in the brain of the two motivations arising out of different sensory inflow, and whether, as Lorenz seems to imply, the resolution of the situation involved some awareness by the fish that it could be about to swallow its offspring along with the worm. Seeking a simple reflex explanation, it might be supposed that the normal inhibiting mechanism stopping the swallowing of a baby fish in the mouth could have supervened and was dominant over the reflex to chew and swallow the worm, and this caused a state of motor paralysis. But the subsequent disgorgement and then separate enactment of the two patterns is rather challenging. It was not that the fish returned to the nest and disgorged both of the objects there, consistent with baby retrieval being dominant, and then it set about eating the worm? It stopped where it was, disgorged, and did the eating first. It then retrieved and delivered the baby to its mother.

Concerning nascent awareness in lower vertebrates and the invertebrates, some remarkable facts have come to light recently from systematic experiment on the learning abilities of octopuses. A salient point is that the findings paralleled what was recounted earlier in the case of dolphins. That is, if one dolphin watched another dolphin perform a complicated trick sequence with several objects, it was sufficient information for the inexperienced dolphin to know how to do it itself. Here the octopus, an invertebrate, was able to learn a task by watching another octopus do it.

Graziano Fiorito and Pietro Scotto made this fascinating study at the Zoological Station of Naples. Individual octopuses learned to discriminate between two balls of similar size but different in colour (red or white). Attacking the correct coloured ball resulted in a small piece of fish as a reward. Attacking the wrong ball caused the animal to be punished by an electric shock. The first group of octopuses, called demonstrators, learned which ball to attack, and training was considered completed when the animals made no mistakes in five trials. A trial lasted about 40 seconds and the intertrial interval was five minutes. Then untrained octopuses, called observers, were housed in an adjacent tank with full visibility and were allowed to watch four trials in which the demonstrators attacked the right ball even though the demonstrators were not rewarded for making the correct response. Video recordings showed the observer octopuses increased attention and followed the demonstrators with their eyes during the four trials. They spent more time outside their homes and displayed other behaviours seen in *Octopus vulgaris* when in the presence of a member of the same species. Thereupon the observer octopuses were given five trials of the procedure. They made the right choice of ball as was done by the demonstrators, even though no reward was given the observers for the right choice. The outcome is that an octopus can learn a task by observing for a short period of time the behaviour of a conspecific. Octopuses watch and octopuses can do! Furthermore, the learning was stable, since it persisted with trials carried out over five consecutive days. Observation is therefore a powerful mechanism of learning.

Such copying of a model in an invertebrate, in the experimenters' view, appears related to the cognitive abilities of the learning system of vertebrates. One interesting question that comes to mind with this fascinating data is whether the same learning would occur if the demonstrators were not conspecifics. There was no mixing of water between the two tanks during the observation phase. Thus, does the exclusively visual appraisal carry any implication of cognition by the octopuses that this was done by one of themselves? After all, presumably they have to know something of this sort in terms of configuration in order to mate?

A Frenchman who has hunted with hounds in the forests and lake area of Bordeaux during the past 50 years has told me the following story in response to the question of an animal's awareness when being pursued. A buck, noted and well known for exceptional antlers, was pursued by hunters and hounds to a lake but then disappeared. The hounds arrived some minutes behind the buck and there were many trees. The dogs had lost it as, of course, there was no scent to follow in the water. Some time later the same chase and sequence occurred and again the animal escaped. On a third occasion the same thing happened at the lake, and the animal triumphed once again. But this time a member of the hunt team, who had dropped out of the chase because of illness, was returning to base by another route and, by chance, encountered the buck emerging 3 kilometres upstream from a river which ran into the lake. The river was shallow, and the animal had run up the bed. On the fourth occasion the huntsmen were waiting for him there. In response to my question, the Frenchman answered: 'I was young then—now I would have let him go.' The view was that the buck, an animal with a sensory world dominated by smell, knew that once it was in water it ceased to provide the telltale basis for the hounds to follow. Alternative to any explanation involving cognition along such lines, a simpler and perhaps more plausible explanation would be that the animal by chance took to water the first time and the sequence it followed removed the threat, and it learned the sequence which had been rewarding. Alternatively, a survival advantage may have accrued for those hunted creatures which entered water as part of an evasion strategy. Indeed, this is a recognised behaviour with buck that are pursued. The animal was simply manifesting genetically programmed behaviour. Thus, in this instance, one might discount any cognitive interpretation, and propose an admixture of genetic propensity and learning without invoking any cognitive element.

Dr Lewis Thomas has expressed eloquently his sense, shared by many scientists, of the prospect of the emergence of the complete novel brain science of the future.

> I do not believe for a minute we are nearing the end of human surprise, despite reasonably put arguments by wonderfully informed scientists who tell us that after molecular biology and astrophysics, there is very little more to learn of substance. Except, they always add, for the nature of human consciousness, and that, they always add, is placed beyond our reach by the principle of indeterminancy; that is, our thought is so much at the centre of life that it cannot sit still while we examine it. But there may be a way out of this; it may turn out that consciousness is a much more generalized mechanism, shared round not only among ourselves but with all the other conjoined things of the biosphere. Thus, since we are not, perhaps so absolutely central, we may be able to get a look at it but we need a new technology for this kind of neurobiology; in which case we will likely find that we have a whole eternity of astonishment stretching out ahead of us.

## SCANNING TECHNIQUES TO LOCATE SITES OF BRAIN ACTIVITY

In our overview and discussion of the events in the brain that are determinant of consciousness, it is paramount to relate that there has been in these past two decades a spectacular revelation of the way the processes of perceiving and thinking are physico-chemical brain events. This ability to see the brain of a conscious person in action comes from imaging techniques, including the positron emission tomography

166

technique (PET for short). It makes images of events inside the skull.

Briefly, the method allows seeing the utilisation of energy which comes from brain cell activity. When a region is active, glucose is burned, carbon dioxide released, and blood flow increases. There is, in a way, a 'blushing' of brain areas, just like the skin blushes when active. In the PET technique where radioisotopes of, for example, carbon or fluorine are injected into blood going to the brain, positrons are emitted there. They collide with electrons to release photons, or particles of light, which a camera outside the skull detects. The particles are richest in those areas where blood flow is greatest, and thus it allows a map of where blood flow and neural activity is greatest. It should be said that because positrons often travel millimetres before collison, the images are not sharp but the localisation is clear enough. Consistent with a vast body of preceding anatomical and neurophysiological knowledge, it is found that when the subject is hearing music, the appropriate regions in the lobe of the brain beneath the right temporal bones light up; when speaking, the speech centre on the left side of the brain lights up; when looking at an object, the region at the back of the brain, known to serve vision, is activated; and so on. But of the greatest importance when the subject is thinking in a darkened silent room as, for example performing the task of counting back from 100 in 7s—a test, incidentally, the neurologists tend to use for early detection of Alzheimer's disease—parts of the frontal cortex, the so-called association areas, light up. Focusing of attention, such as the anticipation by the subject that he or she will shortly be touched upon the index finger, is claimed to cause discrete activation of the brain region that would receive the stimulus. If a subject listens to a language that is understood, particular association areas in the cortex light up, whereas if the language is foreign and there is no understanding of it, this process does not occur. Dr Richard Restak, the Washington neurologist, makes the amusing suggestion that in this way one could detect a spy who denied knowledge of the particular language.

Thus different parts of the brain light up according to what the subject is asked to imagine, or the nature of the sensory inflow coming into the head. The predominant activity of the frontal and prefrontal areas of the brain associated with thinking processes is consistent with the great development of this part of the brain in human beings relative to apes and lower animals. There is a great body of medical knowledge of the profound intellectual effects of damage to these lobes.

A recent study by Per Roland of the Karolinska Institute in Stockholm, a pioneer in this field, and Dr Seitz of Germany, has thrown light on learning of skilled motor performance. It is, for example, a commonplace observation that total concentration is needed to learn sequences such as how to drive a car, change gear, observe lights and other vehicles, but once all this is thoroughly mastered the subject can drive to work on, as it were, 'automatic pilot' and think about events in the coming day. The scientists have studied by PET scan the initial learning, the advanced learning and then mastery of a task involving, in this case, complicated sequences of finger movements. Of course, the major motor and sensory areas in the cortex subserving the fingers were activated at all stages— during learning, or with mastery and thus approaching automatic. One essential element of data emerging from the PET scanning of the three stages of learning (without recounting here in detail the various brain structures operating) was that some areas of the parietal and frontal cortex which had increases of blood flow in the initial stages of learning had reductions in flow as mastery of the task emerged. This change was attributed to the fact that the initial sensory feedback processing and the internal language activations required for learning disappeared when the subject knew how to do it.

Dr Richard Restak, who was the author of an outstanding TV series on the brain and the mind, suggests an intriguing hypothetical situation, where a scientist studying the brain is able to study his or her own PET scan as it is happening, in real time—something not yet possible. In one sense, I suppose, as perceived reality, there could be some analogy to looking at yourself in a mirror and being aware of yourself and reflecting on your own existence. However, in case of the PET scan, to watch the shifting pattern of illuminated areas in your own brain as your attention changed, and your intentions (or will to do things) altered, would be cause for great wonder. On analogy of ape and the mirror, it would be like fingering otherwise inaccessible parts of one's own mind. I imagine the informed or scientific cognoscenti could deliberately think of something on the prediction that an elected area would come alight as one did it, indicating the incontrovertible organic–physical nature of events which somehow, unbeknown to our current scientific analysis, create our awareness, our sense of self and will, or any other of a myriad of conscious sensations. But, as the distinguished Johns Hopkins neuroscientist Vernon Mountcastle has said, PET scanning tells us the where, and how things are linked together, but not how it all works.

## STRUCTURAL DEVELOPMENT OF THE BRAIN

As a matter of fact it is probable that the number of neurones involved in any fleeting mental state is hundreds, thousands or millions, and delineation of what happens in a thought process will be astronomically difficult because all sorts of assemblies will temporarily combine, as indeed shown by PET scanning during thought processes. Jean-Pierre Changeaux remarks: 'It will be such recombining of assemblies of neurones, some with high levels of spontaneous oscillatory activity, which will be the substrate of imagination and the generation of hypotheses.'

Gerald Edelman, Nobel laureate, in his concept called neural Darwinism, sees the brain as dynamically organised into individual networks of neurones that develop differently in individuals during intrauterine existence. Then, as a result of actual life experience after birth, processes will operate differently to select, in a Darwinian sense, advantageous combinations. It will make it more probable that a particular population of cells will be utilised in a future circumstance. Thus a secondary repertoire is superimposed on the primary repertoire established during life in the womb. Rather curiously, this process of brain development involves the death of neurones and regression of surface processes at the same time as cell multiplication and development of connections is going on. There are many more cells and connections during late uterine life, and redundancy is corrected with development.

The outcome is a vast variety of neural combinations, many of which carry out complex activities outside our immediate awareness. As indicated earlier, Michael Gazzaniga sees this picture as that of a great number of modules which subserve a diverse menu of functions but with an interpreter module which does the talking on behalf of the brain. This talking module gives to the whole the perceived sense of unity or self, but often with a tenuous, or indeed, no awareness at all of processes in other modules which actually are determining the behaviour of the person. In one sense, a strong vindication of this modular notion arises with language. I have described how a stroke in a bilingual person or polyglot may wipe out one language, but leave another—perhaps the more recently learned—intact. Parallel to this, when the surface of the brain is being stimulated in a conscious multilingual patient undergoing neurosurgery, and the patient is being asked to name objects shown to him, stimulation in an area may abolish ability to name it in one language but not in another.

A few decades ago the science of the brain was somewhat dominated by behaviourism, which did provide a discipline for the gathering of valuable data. It did this by confining itself to a strictly objective physical explanation of behaviour. A stimulus engendered a response, and whereas internal states might increase the response, as might past experience of reward, there was exclusion of conscious awareness and goals. Consideration of any subjective processes was seen to open the way for intrusion of the dualist viewpoint and, consequently, what, in quite another context, Roger Sperry has termed supernatural, extraphysical, paranormal, unembodied agents which challenge some of the fundamental precepts of science. But, as it became clear to the large majority of neuroscientists that consciousness was inextricably a brain process, the nature of it had to be addressed in studies of behaviour.

I will turn now to two current and radically different theories of the nature of consciousness.

## THE ECCLES HYPOTHESIS

Sir John Eccles has proposed a hypothesis of brain–mind interaction which is set out in his recent book *The Evolution of the Brain: Creation of the Self.* The theory is not simple for the layperson (or, for that matter, the scientist), and some detail is appended as a footnote. Central to the notion is the remarkable architecture of the mammalian cortex whereby there is a bundling of the dendrites or processes of neurones of the lower layers of the cortex as they extend up to the surface layer. This in effect gives, in his view, a functional entity he terms a 'dendron'.

The theory is that mind–brain interaction is accounted for by unitary linkage of hypothetical mental units he terms 'psychons' to these dendrons. A mental intention which is an immaterial phenomenon would act through a psychon. Thus the will effects an action. Conversely, in the transaction from brain to mind, a unitary dendron—for example, in the visual part of the cortex—would act across the interface to its linked psychon to give, say, a red sensation. These independently existing psychons, by virtue of having links to one another, could contrive a moment-to-moment integration of their millions of mental perceptions to give the global or unitary experiences we enjoy. This world of mental events has an existence as autonomous as the world of matter–energy itself does.[*]

---

[*]  How is this all supposed to work?

These dendrons are seen as microunits composed of about 200 neurones which will have about 100 000 synapses or transmitting units on their spines, and there are about 40 million such microunits or dendrons in the human cerebral cortex.

A neurone is excited by special transmitter molecules passing across a cleft or synapse. The idea is that these structures at the synapse (vesicles containing these transmitters) are so extremely small that opening a channel involves the displacement of a particle of about $10^{-18}$ gram.

Thus, these microsites can be operated analogously to the probability fields of quantum physics which have neither mass nor energy, and Heisenberg's uncertainty principle. This, Eccles proposes, has been described by the quantum physicist Margenau.

The work required to initiate the extrusion of the transmitter molecules could be paid back at the same time and place by escaping transmitter molecules from a high to a low concentration. So the transaction of extrusion, or exocytosis, could involve no violation of the conservation laws of physics. The mind would not be called upon to furnish energy. The mental intention would, however, need to activate many hundreds of thousands of vesicles in synapses in this way to actually effect a change in the pattern of neuronal activity.

Eccles' hypothesis, recounted here in a much abbreviated form, has been criticised by J.Z. Young. Specifically, he quotes Eccles' statement about the vesicles containing transmitter molecules at the clefts (synapses)—'the vesicular grid provides *the chance* [sic] for the mental intention to select *by choice* [sic] the exocytosis of a vesicle from a bouton.'

. Young says that presumably the mental intention is clever enough to choose a large enough number of psychons to excite (say) a face cell. [This is a cell dedicated to configuration perception—recognition of features.] He adds: 'Most people will object that it is not legitimate to introduce quantum theory in this way; quantum changes occur, as Eccles himself says, by chance and cannot be directional.'

Young suggests the solution Eccles wants us to adopt is that in birds and mammals there is an agency called the 'mind' (or 'soul') which can perform the holistic feat of 'reconstructing the picture'. For most biologists it will seem unlikely that some special mental process is needed for vision in birds and mammals—but not in reptiles, amphibia or fishes or even in bees and octopuses as Eccles implies. Eccles does not provide any indication of when this facility was conferred. Young concludes that 'the serious and difficult problems of science and philosophy are presented in a stimulating book' but that Eccles' statements will give comfort to religious fundamentalists all over the world. The fact they come from a distinguished student of neurophysiology should not be taken to mean that they are generally, or even widely, accepted.

SPERRY'S IDEA OF MENTALISM

Roger Sperry has put forward a quite different view. The kernel of the idea is that subjective experience, as a gradually emerging outcome of brain evolution, plays a primary guiding role in the actual control of brain function—as, for example, in the flow of patterns of cerebral excitation as revealed by PET screening. The conscious mind is seen to be primary, as a causal agent. Sperry sees evolution as having added this new force. To illustrate this, he suggests that a molecule in many respects is the matter of its inner atoms and electrons. The latter are hauled and forced about in chemical interactions by the overall configuration of the molecule. But if the given molecule is part of a single-celled organism like an amoeba it is, in turn, obliged with all its parts and partners to follow along a trail of events in time and space determined by the overall performance of the amoeba. When it comes to brains, all the simpler electric, atomic, molecular and cellular forces and laws are there. But they are superseded by the configurational forces of higher mechanisms. The processes of cognition, perception and reason, as operating forces, outclass the inner chemical forces. *The organisational interaction within neural hierarchies generating consciousness transcend the physiological as the latter transcends the molecular and it, in turn, the atomic and subatomic.* The cognitive forces exert downward interactive control over organised hierarchies of physiological constituents. Correspondingly we can see there can be an upward control. The conscious processes can be determined and attention forced by events lower in the physiological hierarchy, such as hunger pains from the empty stomach or a full bladder. A will or desire to specific action is set in train. Sperry sees his idea of consciousness, with its power to determine the venue of cerebral excitation as the peak of the hierarchy of brain functions, as a monistic idea. It is quite contrary to the notion of mind as an extra-physical ghostly intervention at the synapses—'the dualistic otherworldly view of Eccles'. In his overview, Sperry rejects also the reductionist view that brain function can be reduced to nothing but its parts and, furthermore, the essence of anything can be sought in its components—although it obviously helps enormously to know of what anything is composed.

The idea of Sperry of interaction in neural hierarchies or nets generating qualities and processes that transcend the physiological entities and are generative of consciousness gives a vision of consciousness as an emergent novel quality. Maybe this has some analogy, in a rough way, to Julian Huxley, H.G. Wells and G.P. Wells' proposal concerning the electric eel described in chapter 1. That is, a characteristic inherent in the function of all living tissues can be elaborated spectacularly and in a manner to give an emergent which is qualitatively quite unique.


THE ULTIMATE RIDDLE


Of course, there remains a yawning chasm between present knowledge and any actual understanding of how the stream of consciousness works. Certainly we can manipulate the stream by experiment, as mentioned earlier, when, for example, unbeknown to a patient having an intravenous infusion, concentrated sodium chloride is injected into the blood, and thirst is immediately evoked. We know from animal experiments when water drinking is rapidly evoked this way that it can be correlated with changes in electrical firing of particular brain cells and the turning on of expression of specific genes in the brain—the proto-oncogenes.

But it presently seems utterly illusive, in relation to Karl Popper's dictate of need of a testable hypothesis, to frame an experiment to actually determine what is happening to the stream of awareness. It is changed, insofar as a compelling urge has surfaced, but what actually is changing in a determinate material sense is profoundly mysterious.

With Sir John Eccles' idea of psychons, immaterial entities which by their linking together give the mind and our global experience, it seems, at least to me, that Elizabeth of Palatine's objection to Descartes remains paramount. That is, to use the alcohol instance again, it deranges not only those functions that could be attributed to the so-called liaison brain—speech, etc., in this scenario—*but the actual quality and content of what the mind would have the talking faculty actually convey*. The putative immaterial entity is just as deranged. To say, as Descartes did, and Sir John seems to in our discussion, that this is a penalty the mind pays for being so intimately associated with the brain, gets vanishingly close to the viewpoint that the mind or conscious thought is what the brain does. That is, the hypothesis has been, in fact, tested in the Popper sense, and it is found that the mind, not just the speech faculty, is deranged by a specific chemical change in the body.

It seems to me plausible that one major selective force, which could have favoured the emergence of dim awareness and consciousness, is the compelling need in lower animals to cross-match data coming in from different sensory organs in order to arrive at or synthesise a coherent picture and then reaction to events in the external world, and thus survive. That is, making the separate information flowing in from, say, touch and sight, or sight and smell and sound, congruent. This imperative to put it together is consonant with what the inspired electrophysiological studies of visual perception in higher animals have revealed. That is, there is parallel processing of inflow in quite different parts of the brain—as, for example, beautifully shown by Dr Semir Zeki of University College, London. Different parts are involved in processing colour or movement; and indeed, as Colin Blakemore, the Oxford neurophysiologist and author of the entralling book *The Mind Machine*, records, there are some twenty different brain areas involved in processing visual input. The knowledge about humans from PET scanning during thinking and word-manipulation, and during learning tasks as described earlier, emphasises that complex mental process involve activity of numerous separate brain areas contemporaneously. A veritable society of neural populations are cooperatively involved in somehow putting the ephemeral picture together in consciousness, including the apogee of the process where the cerebral processes scrutinise themselves and applaud or scorn the activities of the self.

This ultimate of riddles may remain unsolved by biomedical science for centuries. This is not, to use Richard Dawkins' splendid phrase, 'an affirmation of incredulity', such as anti-Darwinians have made in contemplating the evolution of complex structures such as the eye, but simply an intuition as to the complexity of the challenge. Whereas brain imaging gives increasing comprehension of where things happen, Sperry's picture of the subjective as the pinnacle of the hierarchies highlights that some utterly novel and hitherto inconceivable principle or process may emerge to advance our insight. Eschewing solipsism, the enigma is underlined by the great abyss between our confident feelings about what we ourselves picture, feel, desire and think, and what we are able to infer about the outside world from the words, expressions and actions of fellow humans and, at a lower level, the gestures, expressions and behaviour of other animals.

Animals appear to have perceptive awareness at a level that permits images of the outside world and a plan. The mirror experiments with apes tell us of the eventual dawning of self-awareness, but it is an enormous gap between a chimp examining a red spot on its brow and the zenith of human introspection reflected in poetry, drama and philosophy. If brain evolution has crossed this gap in five million years, one may indeed wonder what may develop in the next million if *Homo sapiens sapiens* survives. In any case it has to be contemplated that if ever physiological science gave us a methodology to follow exactly what the brain of a fellow human being was thinking as it was happening, it seems pretty certain that human society would not survive it.

# Appendix

*Dr Miriam Rothschild FRS*

Dr Mirian Rothschild is the daughter of Charles Rothschild who, as well as his banking activities, had a great interest in natural history and assembled a collection of 30 000 specimens of fleas. The family tradition of vast enthusiasm for and knowledge of natural history was exemplified also by her uncle, Walter, who assembled the world-famous collection of two and a quarter million butterflies and moths, 300 000 bird skins and 200 000 birds' eggs. A sizeable section of the bird collection now resides in the American Museum of Natural History. He was renowned for his four-in-hand pulled by zebras, and his collection of giant tortoises.

Miriam Rothschild's early life was immersed in this great zoological tradition and led to her becoming a distinguished entomologist. She is the leading authority in the world on fleas, having written large numbers of papers and books, including the seven volumes of the illustrated catalogue of the Rothschild collection

of fleas published by the Trustee of the British
Museum—co-authored with G.H.E. Hopkins. Her discoveries included the manner in which the reproductive cycle of the rabbit flea is governed by the
hormone cycle of the host animal.

In collaboration with Nobel laureate Professor
Reichstein she showed that the monarch butterfly
stored the cardiac glycoside ingested from the food
plant. It had been surmised for a hundred years, and
their findings opened a new and wide field of research.

Apart from her work in many other fields of entomology and on bird behaviour, she has been a major
force in preserving the wildflower heritage of the
British Isles. She has been deeply involved in important social and political issues, including the provision
of sanctuary for refugees from Nazi Germany, the
legalisation of homosexuality, the introduction of
safety methods in transport, including crash helmets

and safety belts (which she invented), and research into schizophrenia. Ashton Wold, her home, is a sanctuary for a large herd of the rare Père David deer, and the residence of numerous other wildlife in its forests. Perhaps one of her greatest services to science has been by virtue of making her home an international intellectual salon, where people from diverse scientific disciplines, philosophy and humanitities have met together and been catalysed by her vast range of interests and scholarship.

TRANSCRIPT OF A DISCUSSION WITH
DR MIRIAM ROTHSCHILD AT ASHTON WOLD,
PETERBOROUGH, UK, OCTOBER 1990.

DD:   Well, one of the particular problems in this area is to have an operational definition of consciousness in animals. Self-evidently, they can't actually talk to us. And Christopher Longuet Higgins proposed that a creature which shows that it has intentions or a goal could be said to have a mind. It is implicit that it is forming an internal model of the world. Do you think it is a reasonable starting point for a definition of mind in an animal?

MR:   Yes, I do, but I think at the same time that it is awfully difficult for us to interpret animal behaviour correctly because it is so difficult to make the allowance for that extra sensibility, their finer senses in so many areas. We are apt to misinterpret that.

DD:   You mean they can hear at a higher range than we can? They live in a black and white world apparently, in the case of dogs.

MR:   Yes, where the hearing is concerned, the fact that they can tell the difference between the sound of the wheels on your car and any other car, which to them is just as individual as you are yourself, is confusing to us.

DD: Could you give me a specific instance?

MR: Yes, I can give you several. For instance, when I lived at Oxford the road from the high road to Elsfield, where my house was, was tortuous, and it took about ten minutes by car to go from the main road to my house. My secretary thought that the dogs had second sight because she didn't know when I was arriving but she was always alerted by the fact that the dogs went to the door and sat down in the hall waiting for me for ten minutes before I arrived. She thought the dogs had second sight, but I am convinced that they could hear the wheels of my car and identify it far off, when it began that tortuous road. This particular thing of being able to interpret which car was which by the sound of wheels—the answers are really outside our capacities. We really don't do that. I mean, when a car arrives we don't really know who it belongs to, but the dogs do. You could misinterpret that. It was interesting that when the old bitch began to go deaf, she didn't walk to the door with the other dogs.

*The next section of discussion has been incorporated into chapter 3.*

DD: Have you observed emotions in animals that in your view have given rise to a particular form of behaviour that can be interpreted as anticipation or expectancy? I am thinking, for example, of one instance cited by Professor Thorpe of Cambridge at a conference, where he pointed out an observation of Professor Hinde and Miss Spencer Booth on a colony of monkeys. They had a male and several females in each colony and they had an outdoor compartment and an indoor compartment with a window between the two. With the females, there were dominant females and subordinate females. What happened—one of the lower subordinate females had an infant which appeared to be very attractive to the superior female monkey. On two occasions she actually got hold of the infant and it had to be restored to the rightful mother. Then, when the mother went inside the room, the dominant female came up and started making noises at the window, and then leapt back as if it had been attacked by the subordinate female inside, thereupon the dominant male went inside and beat up the subordinate female. This was done several times. Professor Thorpe interpreted this as a clear procedure where the animal expected a consequence of its act—punishment of the subordinate. I am wondering, in relation to the issue of jealously between animals, whether you have observed anything that might be interpreted as expectancy?

MR: No, I can't really say I have thought about that. But there was one very, very funny episode in my life with animals which I have never really been able to interpret. I had to control in a sense my feeling that it was—I didn't want to be anthropomorphic about it—it is rather a long story, but I must explain it to you.

In the garden underneath the house where I lived, very close to the house was a pond, and on this pond were two ducks. They had a nest there. The pond was surrounded by a tiny little wood, a little cover, and in this cover there lived a fox. The fox and the ducks had come to some sort of understanding, because the fox never really attacked the ducks. But when the fox went back to its lair too near the pond, the ducks used to give an alarm quack which was clearly to be heard in the house. When they gave the alarm quack my dogs, which were in the house, knew that the fox was passing through the wood and used to rush out and chase it. When this happened there was no doubt about it that the clue to the fox being there was the quacking of the ducks.

Now the story becomes much more complicated. I had a tame magpie that was a wonderful mimic. It could mimic other birds, and it appeared to me that it would take an enormous amount of pleasure in teasing my dogs in various ways—it imitated, for instance, the charlady coming in who used to say 'Morning', and the dogs instantly used to get up and come and meet the charlady who wasn't there. Now this magpie learnt that if it imitated the quacking sound of the ducks that the dogs rushed into the garden, and many a time I have seen this magpie try this trick on the dogs and they shot off the bed down into the garden to this imaginary fox. I could never, never get out of my head that the magpie amused itself like this, and it must have anticipated in some way. It was almost impossible not to think that that magpie got some satisfaction out of this. It must have somehow collected all its facts together. Well it is just one of those anecdotes which, as Dr Thorpe said, you couldn't really explain.

DD:   He also told one at the Vatican Conference on Consciousness—an extraordinary interesting story about yourself and an owl that seemed to me to be an instance of a change in a demeanour of an animal which was feasible to interpret as emotion.

MR:   Complete jealousy.

DD:   Could you tell us what happened with that?

MR:   Well, I had a barn owl which I reared—it was blown out of its nest—and by a curious coincidence at that time I was expecting a child and I was bedridden because they anticipated that I was going to have a miscarriage. I lay on my back in bed for about three months and during that time I enjoyed the fact that I had got this baby barn owl in a waste paper basket at the bottom of my bed. We developed a very, very close relationship and this baby barn owl became really completely fixed on me—I mean, I was its mother. The doctor who used to come to visit was always very astonished when suddenly out of the bottom of the basket on the end of the bed a barn owl popped up, because, of course, by the end of three months it was feathered. It then continued to live with me in my sitting room and was a constant companion, and if I was writing at my desk it used to come and sit on my lap and expect to be tickled and petted. It used to close its eyes in ecstasy when you rubbed it under the chin and so forth. It was very, very tame. Then the baby I had been expecting was born. I went away to London to have the baby in the hospital, and when I returned the barn owl's demeanour towards me had changed dramatically. Instead of the friendly animal it used to be, it attacked me very viciously and struck at my face and behaved as if I was a great enemy. It didn't behave like that to any other people in the house. It was only directed towards me, and I was very frightened that it would attack the baby. We had a net over the baby's pram and so forth, but it was relentless and I could not believe that this animal who had been so close to me, so friendly, more friendly than a cat, would suddenly turn against me in this traumatic fashion.

I used to think I could overcome it, that it would return to earlier form. I used to, to everyone's amusement, sit indoors with a helmet on my head to protect myself—it was just after the war and, of course, this was a helmet one wore as an air raid warden. I used to sit there with this helmet on and a net over my face. No, it was relentless. I had to give it away because I couldn't overcome this sudden change of behaviour.

DD: On the issue of expectancy in animals, a very interesting case is cited, again by Professor Thorpe. Some experiments were done on rhesus monkeys where the animal was trained to observe a piece of food being put under one of several inverted containers. A piece would be put under the one container and then, after a period, the animal was allowed access. With almost unerring accuracy it would go to the one under which the food had been placed. Then they did an experiment whereby after placing the food they put a shade in front of the containers for a short period. Thereupon the banana that had been put under there was removed and a piece of lettuce leaf was put in its place. Then the screen was taken away and the animal was allowed in, and it immediately went to the correct container, turned it over, saw the lettuce leaf which normally it would eat, and discarded it. Actually on some occasions it threw a temper tantrum. This seemed on the face of it to be consistent with the fact that the animal had an expectancy in relation to what it would find—what it liked most—banana. Therefore, emotion was invoked by not finding what it expected. Regarding expectancy in animals in that regard, you did, of course, have the collie dog with a plan to get the labrador off the chair.

MR: Expectancy? Yet again, I have a feeling that if I had been aware of this story I would probably be able to produce several episodes like this but I can't actually recall one which was really comparable to that.

DD: I suppose in the terms of an automaton you could design a computer that would throw a tantrum when it got an answer it didn't foresee, but it is difficult...

MR: As I think I mentioned to you before, if you live very closely with animals as I do, and they are very close companions, and share one's life in a sense, in a way it almost exaggerates their resemblance to one's self. One exaggerates it really, I think in one's own mind, but at the same time so many small episodes happen which you don't actually recall, but which certainly give you the impression that in a minor key the animal resembles yourself. This is why I think the thing really comes through. It is always on a minor key—rather like my relationship with my grandchildren. You feel that the animal in so many small ways responds, but I do think one thing—I think we all underestimate the animal's appreciation of the finer details of the environment, and this may lead you to an anthropomorphic attitude.

I mean, I can give you an example, a very odd example—I'm not saying this has anything to do with intelligence. On the contrary, it is the finer appreciation of detail. My collie dogs are very similar in appearance to foxes, and when I kept the foxes when they were very tame, one or two of them used to walk around the garden with me at the same time as the collie dogs—used to go around all in a bunch. Now, the swallows flying at a very great height in the air could always tell the difference between the collie dogs and the foxes. If the foxes walked with me despite the fact that collies have the same sort of tail, the same sort of markings, the same sort of colour, more or less to our eye, the swallows would dive bomb when there were foxes out there. They would come screaming down and dive bomb. It struck me how superior their eyesight was that they could differentiate at that height and moving at that speed between a fox and one of my collie dogs. This episode was one of those that brought home very strongly that we don't appreciate how finely tuned all these animals are, and consequently misinterpret their behaviour very much.

DD:   In terms of acting to a plan and having a clear intent, perhaps one of the most interesting instances are those studies that have been done on the Arctic wolves up in Ellsmere Island—which is 500 to 1000 miles from the nearest tree. They live in caves and so on. These creatures have been followed very closely on film, and they accept humans in their environment after a period of time—biologists have spent the entire summer up there with them, watching them. But they would set out, often with the alpha male, the leading male, in front, in single file, and travel for something like 20 miles, across a river, until they eventually come to the musk oxen. Then they will fan out—and this was recorded very impressively on film—and attack them. In this case, in the first instance there were three or four rather mature oxen and they, you know, grouped, fought back at the wolves, and after a period of time the wolves gave up. There was resting between periods of attack, but they gave up. One might raise the question of whether there is some sort of value judgment and whether the chance of being damaged exceeds the prospect of getting food.

Then, after that, they set off again in another direction and came across a group of musk oxen which had two calves, and they succeeded after a considerable number of manoeuvres in detaching one of the calves, and then two of the wolves killed that calf while the others went on and endeavoured to detach the other calf.

There was, on the face of it, some evidence of cooperative hunting in that regard. They didn't succeed in detaching the other calf, but they then eventually, of course, ate the calf that had been killed. Then with full bellies they went back to their home base and regurgitated and fed the young pups. But it seemed, on the face of it, they started with a clear intent. Now maybe they had low blood sugars or maybe, in the situation, they could at that distance of 20 miles or more detect the musk oxen, but the evidence was, and which has been seen in areas in Africa, of a cooperative procedure in hunting.

MR: I have seen with my dogs a bit of cooperative hunting. But I have also seen other quite interesting episodes with the collies. There are a lot of grey squirrels here, and again and again the collies chase the grey squirrels and they escape by running up the tree. Now after this had happened many times, the collies changed their strategies. They didn't chase the squirrels on the ground but they sat—literally—they literally sat quite still watching until the squirrels came down off the trees, and then they pounced on them. They reversed the whole process, instead of chasing the squirrels on the ground where they found them, they waited for them to come down. Well, that seemed to me to involve some process of thought.

DD: Expectancy of likely behaviour of the squirrels.

MR: Yes, and also a fitting together the idea that then it was easier to catch them. To wait for them to come down rather than to chase them so that they got up the tree. I was very impressed with that because it involved a change in the dogs' behaviour. Their instinct, of course, is to rush after something—you know, they catch the smell or the sight of a squirrel and off they go. But here they changed their behaviour to fit in with what they thought the squirrels were going to do or what they noticed.

The next section of the discussion on smell and dreaming has been incorporated into chapter 5.

DD: The question of animals lying. Perhaps a very good example of that is the one that has been described by Ruppel with the artic fox. There was a mother with some very well-developed pups and they were competing with her for food. They adopted extremely unpleasant tactics, like urinating in the mother's face, and what the mother used to do after several such instances was give an alarm sound, a warning call, and the young, being programmed to this, would run off and then the mother would seize the food. I mean, she would outwit them. It looked very much like a plan.

MR: Of course, to revert to what I was saying about the dog which was excited by jealousy, then turning and behaving in a nice way to the object of her jealousy. It was a very subtle lie.

DD: Can you tell that story?

MR: Yes, the dog was very jealous of my friendship with a cousin who used to arrive suddenly. She behaved in just a way that dogs behave—if you pat one the other comes rushing up and wants attention. She did that for a bit, and then she conceived this way—I mean, of course, one shouldn't think in human terms, but it appeared that she wanted to get even with me. She turned from trying to attract my attention and love, to lavishing attention herself on the hated object—the cousin. One of the things she did was to get into bed with her and to sit on the bed, and when she did this she would lie down, put her head on her paw and look out of the corner of her eye at me to see what the effect was. This was so obvious and so noticeable that we were very amused by this and we used to set it up just to show the extraordinary bad behaviour on the part of the dog.

DD: That issue of expressions—of course, Darwin covered it very fully in the *Expression of Emotion in Man and Animals*. Of course, he seemed to have no doubt that dogs had emotions.

MR: Oh, yes ... I don't know how you relate emotions to consciousness, that's a different thing.

DD: Do think you can have an emotion without being conscious? An angry bee?

MR: Oh yes, I think you can if you call it an emotion. Yes you can, definitely. But what is interesting about the dogs is that they have finer emotions. You can differentiate, I mean it is not just anger, pleasure and so forth, but they are much more subtle forms of emotion in dogs. I have no doubt at all they have emotions, but I wouldn't dare commit myself that they were conscious simply because they exhibit emotions.

DD: There is one interesting thing in terms of, perhaps, a creature dissembling—I have had one experience of that sort. As we have said, everybody has their own animal pet, and obviously all such things are open to considerable suspicion in terms of anthropomorphising. I had, I think, a very intelligent dachshund by the name of Osbert, and I remember I was sitting one day up on the bed having my lunch with a tray and eating a sausage. About half the sausage was on the plate, and the dog came up in a very casual manner and jumped on the bed, just looked around and paid no particular attention. It looked out of the window, and then suddenly turned sideways, grabbed the sausage off the plate, leapt down and went hurtling down the stairs. Now obviously, if it had just put its snout across towards the sausage it would have got tapped, firmly, and told to disappear. But it seemed as if, retrospectively, that the dog had appraised the situation and actually had a plan. Clearly the disappearance down the stairs and to considerable distance outside indicated that it would have to put a distance between it and me to avoid having the sausage taken from it. I mean, again, anthropomorphising, but it was difficult to presume that the sequence of events was not associated with some intent, and the execution of a plan.

MR: One of the difficulties in interpreting animal behaviour, is that one doesn't know the steps which lead up to a certain sort of behaviour. I mean, I was very worried by the wounded partridge stunt. Do you know when the partridge has a nest and wants to lead you away from it, it pretends it's got a broken wing, and trails the wing, and runs in the opposite direction. That worried me always to interpret that—and then, of course, a lot of research was done on the various situations which lead up to that. With your thing with the dog bolting off down the stairs, I don't know if you have noticed, but if a dog is given something that is a bit too large for it to swallow, it doesn't attempt to eat it on the bed with you but it always walks off a little way with it—under the table or something, and those are the sorts of things you presumably have to ask yourself—what is the build up of any form of sudden behaviour?

DD: Yes, I agree. I suppose the velocity with which it went—which obviously had the suggestion of escape—would be something to do with it. I take it with the partridge, since many partridges show this behaviour, one would have to presume that it is a genetically preprogrammed evasive method with the partridge, and could occur without any conscious response to the stimulus.

MR: But it's misleading, it's the sort of thing which could mislead you if you are not very much aware of that sort of thing.

DD: Sure.

MR: But the genetic element in behaviour—that's the thing which is difficult to interpret isn't it?

DD: Yes.

MR: Sensory acuity—and genetic programming combined can lead you up the garden path.

DD: Yes, I mean it is obvious there can be quite a substantial sequence of events involved in a genetic programming and, of course, it may embody the propensity to learn certain things. I think one very good example of genetic programming that I read of recently that I wasn't aware of was Galen's experiment where a goat was delivered by caesarian section of a kid, and when the kid was just put on the floor and shaking the amniotic fluid off itself, a series of bowls were then presented which contained sugars and sweet things and oats. One contained milk and the little kid just born went across to the milk and started. Of course Galen and his colleagues cheered. I mean it's consistent with that idea of Marais that every creature is born with the knowledge of the food it is constitutionally meant to eat. The koala somehow knows, if that is the correct term, under genetic programming that it is destined to eat gum leaves—eucalyptus leaves—rather than meat or some other forms of food.

MR: Yes, but don't you think that the reverse can also lead you astray? In a sense we are all genetically programmed, yet we have got a mind and can do a great deal with it. I mean you can go too far that way if you attribute everything to genetic programming and finer sensibilities and so forth. Don't forget that we are genetically programmed too and have sensibilities, and yet we can think.

DD: Yes, I agree with you entirely on that.

MR: You know, one would like to have ten lives because there are so many interesting things that you would like to investigate. All sorts—I would love to go back and start again. There's so many observations that one could make. People are not very observant about themselves really, are they? Although the only thing we are really interested in is ourselves. Hence we have a soul! We still don't really watch what's happening.

DD: No, well I suppose as a number of writers have said, whereas it appears to be easy, the process of scrutinising one's own thought processes is extraordinarily difficult in relation to accurately recording and seeking one's own motivations. As Gazzaniga has said in terms of synthesis of his experience with the split-brain patients, he believes that the brain is made up of many modules, one of which can talk, but the others may be powerful in terms of motivation by directing, and in effect, determining the behaviour of the individual. At the same time, of course, the speaking segment of the brain is often called upon to interpret what is being directed in behaviour by other segments of the brain which are mute but, nonetheless, extremely powerful in determination of what happens in the individual.

MR: Of course, as I am old, I am particularly interested, as one is so self-centred, in the changes that take place with age. And one of the things that has interested me very much is that the speed at which things happen is altered. For instance, in the old days if I was going to make myself a cup of tea I'd have made a cup of tea without thinking about it. But when age comes on, you actually segment the thought and say—Now I am going to make myself a cup of tea—and in your mind you see the teapot, you see the tea, you see the sugar, you see the milk as separate entities, whereas before it was just one act and you didn't segment it. This, I think—this is the reason why old people seem to talk to themselves because they no longer think in flashes but actually in words.

DD: Well, that in a way might be construed, if you like to put it that way, as a return to the learning process. I mean, the classic example of this is the situation where in learning to drive a car, all these things are a matter of extreme concentration. You are conscious of them—you learn the sequence—you learn also, not merely the sequence in the car, but the route you take. You become familiar with these things. Several years later, you can do all that on what might be described as automatic pilot. I mean, you can drive to work, go through all these things and you really are not conscious of being there. You are thinking about the events of the day. In a way, it is almost like the split-brain situation which is contrived by dividing the commissure. But I suppose what you are suggesting is that at certain stages of life, because of diminution of the facility to do these things, you have to go back, in a sense, to the learning stage.

MR:   Well, I have an idea that what happens is everything slows up as you get older, I mean physically speaking. I think the ability to couple everything together in a flash has gone—and you are just back to the original state where you saw them as separate things. I often think, though, as these various episodes occur in my mind, I often think that, well, perhaps animals are like that too. Or they may go even further than we do along the line of synthesising everything together, doing things in a flash. You know, I mean it arouses your interest in the different processes.

DD:   But have you watched changes in the behaviour of animals, and presumptively in their cerebral processes determining same with age, and been struck by this with the behaviour of your animals?

MR:   Yes, they do change with age—very much so. There is a general slowing up. And, just the same— you can't tell which sense has gone but I mean that black and white dog of mine that bit Professor Brakefield yesterday, he was very friendly one moment, and then obviously didn't recognise him the next. You know, I think their eyesight goes, their hearing goes, their smell goes, and everything gets dimmer, and they don't act in the way which one would expect. I think the aging process in animals may be equal to ours. Anyone, I think, who really takes an interest in the aging process and watches these changes can learn an awful lot. Well, you see that's something that I can think of. That dog that was lying on the bed looking out of the corner of its eye. That was humorous.

DD:   Right.

MR: I have seen signs of amusement in dogs.

DD: As distinct from delight of the sort that Darwin described when he headed in the right direction for his dog when they went out for a walk?

MR: Yes, a different thing to that. You see, in order to notice those things in a dog you really have to live with them. You can't observe that every day. This is a thing which comes from really knowing the dog. I have seen them also teasing each other. Not just playing with each other but actually teasing, and watching the effects.

DD: Did you think with this dog that got the labrador out of the chair by bouncing the ball, when it got into the chair it showed any signs of being pleased with itself?

MR: Yes, I think it always looked triumphant. But there again, you see it is so easy to be anthropomorphic. I really thought that, and I also think the dog that I described, you know, the lying animal, when we were talking before—that dog used to show gratitude to certain people, which was different from affection.

DD: How would that be—what would you notice?

MR: It's so difficult to describe it, but it was the attitude of friendliness because it had received some special attention from the person or it had been fed by the person. And it showed appreciation without affection. It's awfully difficult to describe, but if you saw it you would know exactly what is meant. You know, it is very difficult to describe appreciation in a human being—I'll tell you what it was—it was politeness. These dogs were polite to the maids but didn't show real affection. It's very odd that, but that was the fact. I noticed that repeatedly. But it's awfully difficult to describe. But what I would say was, that in my experience with dogs, they have a whole range of emotions which can very easily be associated with our own emotions.

DD: Yes, well, Lorenz, of course, has described considerable differences in dogs. I mean, in his *Man Meets Dog*—those that have come from the Golden Jackal lineage, and those derived from the wolf. The differences are in, I suppose, the attachment to one particular person, and then they realise that the other people are part of that social organisation, but in a way peripheral to the principal person.

MR: I think it is awfully difficult to dissociate what you feel are emotions yourself and which you perceive in the dog—with a more behaviouristic attitude—very difficult to really scientifically separate.

DD: Yes.

MR: But if you live with animals closely you become much more aware of their emotions than if you just casually . . . Well, you would, wouldn't you, with human beings?

DD: In the discussions that occur with regard to whether a computer will be developed with such sophistication that it will simulate to all intents and purposes the mind—Lord Adrian remarked that if we asked it whether it was conscious and it said it was we wouldn't believe it—and Wilder Penfield has raised the question whether any robot could see a joke. He suspects that a sense of humour would be about the last thing that a machine would have. You were mentioning humour in animals a little earlier. I gather at one stage you were involved in an analysis of humour with the famous Arthur Koestler.

MR:   That's right—Arthur asked me to write a book with him as a joint author, and the book was going to be on humour, and I said to him, but Arthur you don't know what humour is—you don't even understand a joke—and he denied this. And I arranged a special dinner party for him at which I invited three or four people I thought were the most amusing people I knew—including Isaiah Berlin and John Foster—and explained to them that they had to try and analyse or explain a joke to Koestler. We had a most hilarious dinner—where John Foster, who was a fabulous raconteur, told one joke after another, and not once did Koestler even smile, and he wrote them down all in longhand even the most disgusting jokes that were produced by John.

DD:   He came out with a great analysis on the sense of humour I think.

MR:   I remember one joke in which he said that a farmer was asked in a verbal driving examination, 'Can you make a U-turn?', and he said, 'No, but I can make them squeal!' Koestler wrote that down in longhand—make a ewe squeal. We laughed so much that we all nearly died, but he never smiled.

DD:   That is one point which would be very interesting in relation to the general issue at stake—the question of imitation in animals—and I believe this has been particularly described in terms of dolphins. The fact that dolphins will actually imitate seals in their tank and lie on their back and kick like seals, but the classic one is the dolphin picking up a feather and actually scraping the window of the tank in the manner that the diver who is accustomed to cleaning the tank did, and also making noises like the escape of air from the demand valve of the aqualung. Others were seen to go along and scrape the bottom of the tank with a bit of shell or tin—again imitating. Now if you imitate, like an actor—one's watching a sequence of events. There has got to be the correct sequence, and there's got to be, in effect, the whole situational thing of how it imitates the behaviour. There must be a plan and an intent involved.

MR: Yes, you see, my wretched magpie that imitated the quack of the duck and the charlady who used to say, 'Good morning Mrs Lane'—it used to have quite a lot of phrases—I mean that was imitating and watching results too. Imitation, I think, is a very important thing.

DD: And a biological advantage in that one can create situations that may be of advantage to the animal imitating.

MR: But of course. I have never really studied it, that's the trouble. I haven't consciously gone out to observe that, but I mean the case of the magpie was startling really. It learnt to quack like this duck when the foxes came back—it imitated so exactly. Now that's another thing—that they got some satisfaction from imitation. Because you know that when you come to the end of a line with a typewriter, a bell rings. Well, that magpie used to imitate that bell very effectively . . . we would say it definitely got a kick out of that. When the woman started typing, it would sound the bell before she got to the end of the line—which was very amusing to watch. I would say the magpie seemed to get some form of satisfaction out of its imitations. Now, for instance talking about imitations, Mrs Busnell had a laboratory which had a large population of small parrots, and these parrots had a peculiarity that they learnt—the males each had an individual song which they sang to the females—they were all quite individual songs. These love birds, they paired for life. They had an epidemic—oh yes, I must explain that the lab was studying these songs so they had tape recordings of each individual male song. They had an epidemic of coccydiosis which left many widows and many widowers. At first they had great difficulty in getting them to mate with a new mate but they did eventually. And then one day somebody played back the song of a deceased male on the gramophone and the female immediately left her own mate and went and stood at the gramophone. She had remembered this song all that time, and still had that association—which was very surprising—I mean that gives rise to a lot of speculation, doesn't it, about memory and all the rest of it in animals?

DD: Yes, I suppose on the other hand it could be interpreted simply as a stimulus of which she had the complete circuits and simply responded to the stimulus independent of the situation it was now in.

MR: Oh absolutely, but I mean they're the sort of things that can confuse the anthropomorphic attitude of the observer who doesn't think along those lines.

DD: Right.

MR: And the lab itself was surprised that this bird remembered, because these songs were quite complicated, and this female had got accustomed to a new song and yet this old one triumphed over the new one—so there were a lot of complications there. I am sorry you didn't see the Busnell laboratory because they had crickets which achieved dominance by early singing—the one that got up first and sang was the one that become dominant and had access to the food.

DD: Dolphins apparently have a language, but I

understand from Dr Griffin that at this point there hasn't been a great deal of success—I mean, they do make sounds and they have been recorded, obviously instruments have followed it in detail—but so far there hasn't been a great deal of success in interpreting just exactly what is communicated.

MR:   No.

DD:   Presumptively, the communication or the emission of sounds and reciprocal sounds wouldn't occur unless there was some purpose to it.

MR:   Busnell told me that their vocabulary was limited, and that he thought 30 words was the maximum he could teach his dolphins. Unfortunately, Busnell is dead so we can't question him on this.

DD:   Parrots, of course, have been proposed to be able to be taught—quite a considerable capacity to distinguish shapes—to know the number of objects in a pile and to report when things are similar or different, and to utilise their small vocabulary that they have in order to signal these things. Also, experiments have been done without the observer that's trained them—they have brought somebody else in—in order to avoid that situation of unconscious transfer of information like in the Clever Hans experiment.

MR:   Well, I have not had that sort of experience with birds. I have kept birds free in my house, and have watched them very carefully but I haven't ever tested them in that sort of way. One thing of course is very deceptive in birds. Some birds have a very good long-term memory, and they can convey information that they have learnt a long time ago to other birds. For instance, I had a crow which was a feral crow—it used to come in for food—and it brought a mate with it after a year but it wouldn't let the mate eat the toxic moths. It actively prevented it. Which I thought was very strange. But that had been observed before by Swynterton with young birds where the mother prevented young birds eating toxic foods.

\* \* \*

*Sir John Eccles FRS*

Sir John Eccles completed his medical studies at the University of Melbourne, Australia, in 1929. He was awarded a Rhodes Scholarship to Oxford University and there worked under Sir Charles Sherrington, the great neurophysiologist. After twelve years of fruitful work at Oxford, he returned to Australia in 1937 to become Director of the Kanematsu Institute at Sydney Hospital where, with Sir Bernard Katz and Dr Stephen Kuffler, major advances in the knowledge of nerve-muscle function were pioneered. In 1944 Eccles took up the Chair of Physiology at the University of Otago, in Dunedin, and during this period in New Zealand his friendship with the philosopher Karl Popper began and flourished. In 1951 he accepted Sir Howard Florey's invitation to become Professor of Physiology in the new John Curtin School of Medical Research at the Australian National University in Canberra. There he created a great school of neurophysiology, attracting workers in this field from all over the world. In 1963 Sir John received the Nobel Prize for his work on ionic mechanisms of synapses. After a period engaged in research work in the United States, at the State University of New York at Buffalo, Sir John moved to live in Switzerland in 1975. Since then he has written extensively on the brain–mind problem,

including the conjoint work with Sir Karl Popper en-titled *The Self and its Brain* (Springer Verlag, 1977) and recently *The Evolution of the Brain: Creation of the Self* (Routledge, London, 1989). The latter embodies a wide-ranging discussion of anthropology and the development of language, and along with his paper entitled 'A unitary hypothesis of mind–brain interaction in the cerebral cortex' (published in the Proceed-ings of the Royal Society, London, 1990) it sets out Sir John's recent theory on the brain–mind interaction.

TRANSCRIPT OF A DISCUSSION WITH SIR JOHN ECCLES, BASLE, SWITZERLAND, SEPTEMBER 1990.

*The first section of the discussion has been incorporated into chapter 3.*

DD:   Getting back to the evolutionary side of it—the

question—at what point in evolution did consciousness emerge? For instance, Wilder Penfield proposed in the Vatican Symposium of 1964 that the indispensable substrate of consciousness lies outside the cerebral cortex, in the brain areas below it, though all regions of the brain are involved in consciousness, and Jeanne Pierre Changeaux likened the reticular activating system, which Penfield is referring to, to the console of an organ which can be played and direct attention to particular areas of the cortex and so on. What I was curious about is, since this area is obviously more primitive—the reticular activating system, from an evolutionary point of view—whether the fact that it plays such a great role in consciousness perhaps is consonant with the fact that there is a dim awareness in animals prior to major development of the cortex? I mean, going back to the reptiles and so on, the fact, phylogenetically, that that capacity is in the reticular activating system and it plays such a crucial role.

JE: I think that Penfield was quite wrong. The centrocephalic system now is eliminated, Sperry will tell you that. He has worked with the split brain and so on. It shows that the whole of Penfield's story has to be abandoned.

DD: What about people that are damaged in that area, as a result of a haemorrhage or something?

JE: Vigil coma it's called when you have some accident, a car accident, which damages that part of the reticular activating system. The cerebral cortex to all appearances after death can look all right, but the higher brain stem area is damaged. I agree with this situation. The interpretation is that it provides a background to keep the cerebral cortex normally working.

If that background is knocked out the cerebral cortex does not normally work and you are unconscious. Hassler tried to stimulate the individual coma cases, and he got some success in recovery this way. Not that the consciousness is there but it provides background, just like the blood supply provides background to the cerebral cortex to give you consciousness. I am very strongly of the opinion that the mammalian cerebral cortex is the sole seat of consciousness. Maybe there is an equivalent in the higher birds, but reptiles and other animals don't measure up at all. And so, then I begin to think in the evolutionary story that consciousness came at the development of the mammalian cerebral cortex which is very special, much more special than we have realised hitherto, wiring up structure where you can begin to get consciousness. This is my story of the mind events operating on the brain. Quantum physics is where you have to be to get into the world of consciousness from the brain. You have got to go through happenings that can only be explained by quantum physics, not by classical physics.

DD: You stated, Jack, that it will be realised that the modern Darwinian theory of evolution is defective in that it does not even recognise the extraordinary problem that is presented by living organisms acquiring mental experiences of a non-material kind, that are in another world from the world of matter/energy. It seems to me that the question of whether mental experiences are in another world from that of matter/energy is at least open. Perhaps there's strong evidence to the contrary, including your own citation of work showing that the cerebral blood flow increases locally in discrete regions of the parietal lobe when, for example, the subject is thinking about a mental arithmetic problem. The radioxenon that is put into the carotid artery shows an increased circulation which shows presumably increased neural activity, so the thought process causes a concurrently demonstrable material/energy event. Would not that be so?

JE:  Yes, that is so, but the thought process doesn't start by itself. It starts as a mental performance. That is, it's your brain and you are suddenly wanting to do mental arithmetic. So you then trigger your brain to do it but that is the thought process which is working—it is your thought in the first place, your decision to want to ask a question like subtract 3 from 50 successively.

DD:  Could you think without the brain to do that—to initiate it?

JE:  No you can't, but on the other hand the brain doesn't do it by itself. The brain can't start to do that without you thinking. It's interaction you see. You're interacting between the brain and mind events. Otherwise you are stuck with materialistic determinism, and none of us want to be just determined that way. We always want to be able to ask questions and discuss and to start new concepts. Just to start some arithmetics or what you will. We're all the time working as the mind, using our brain intimately. You have to admit that your mind or mental processes are the initiators of what happens in all voluntary movements. When I want to move my finger, I can move as I will, and any particular finger I want. But I still have the thought that I am doing it. Penfield's experiment was to stimulate the brain, the motor cortex, and get the subject to move a finger. The subject was saying that I do not do that—you did it to me. He knows the difference between the finger movement that was triggered by an electrical stimulus and a finer movement that he initiated.

DD:   That could still be a function of the brain—that he's intervened at a particular level of a process which is holistic within the brain.

JE:   But you said he's intervened.

DD:   That is with the electrode.

JE:   O, yes—Penfield has intervened there, but then the subject recognises the difference—and he said this is not something that I wanted to do but you did it to me. So he believes that he is thinking he is able to do a finger movement, say, by thought. And that is, of course, a fundamental question. And that is what my theory is about.

*The next section of the discussion has been incorporated into chapter 2.*

DD:   I would like to take another tack. One of the things in your most recent book, which obviously has been a great focus of attention for you, is the rapidity of evolution of the brain over the last four million years. It's increase in size and so on. On this issue of rapid development of the brain, we have the concrete proposal of Lumsden, and E.O. Wilson of Harvard, which they termed gene culture co-evolution. The situation they described is autocatalytic. New forms of behaviour are invented by the brain but the forms are very much influenced by the genes, and a feedback occurs from culture to genes in that success causes the prescribing genes to spread through the population. I'd like to ask you about this in relation to a crucial event in terms of how fast it could accelerate cerebral evolution. I'd like to, say, bring up the discovery of fire and man being able to make it electively. It

appears to have happened with *homo erectus* somewhere, say, 400 000 to about 1.3 million years ago—not
known exactly, but you know, within that area. Perhaps, until then, the hominids were tropical mammals
locked into a twelve-hour day/twelve-hour night cycle,
going to sleep at dusk, just as has been shown for
tropical primates. With the discovery of fire and thus,
you know, light at night, it could have provided a
powerful selection pressure favouring those people
with biological clocks in their brains which weren't
rigidly operative on the twelve-hour cycle. Gathering
around the camp fire in the cave would accelerate the
development of language, it would accelerate the
development of tools and fashioning objects with the
aid of heat, strategies of co-operative hunting, and for
warfare could have increased success, and not least,
and not last, the art of cooking developed with the
vast expansion of nutritional possibilities. I mean you
could render foods that were potentially toxic not
toxic, and you could make them very much more
digestible. Now, these capacities could have been
selected in sequence favouring those brains with cerebral organising capacities in these directions, but I
raise whether the emancipation from the twelve-hour
light/dark cycle in the tropics, as Richter did, might
have been vital for the invasion of Eurasia from
Africa—I mean man having developed on the basis of
palaeontogical evidence as a tropical mammal. So, if
you look at that, there is then the question of whether
you could get small reproductive groups and, in
them—like the Eldredge/Gould hypothesis of specific
quantal jumps in the evolutionary process—you could
get very rapid changes in small populations as a result
of this class of event. I mean, in other words, as
Lumsden and Wilson said, 'Prometheus stole fire from
the Gods and gave its creative power to the human

race'. The Promethian gift was a supreme event in the Hellenic narrative of the origin of man. But I am bringing it up as one of the possible events that really caused great acceleration in the development of the cortex because of the major change in lifestyle, and life events that may have been feasible.

JE:    Yes, I think there may be something in that but surely the great event that came in hominid evolution was language, and language with all the subtlety of ideas being able to be transmitted to others. The way in which you could describe, for example, what you'd seen, where there could be good food or a good hunt or something like that. The operations of the tribe with ability to argue and talk about what should be done.

DD:    That's essentially what I was saying, cultural change.

JE:    The family with the whole societal relationships. I agree with all that, but it came from language, I think. And why do I think that? Because this was earlier than you say with fire. We do know the sizes of the brain and that the Australopithicenes with 450 cc or so got increased to 650 cc with *Homo habilis*. Now this increase came fairly sharply, and it could only have been explained on evolutionary terms by the necessity that language required more subtle brain performance and, only in the evolutionary process, those with larger brains were more able to develop the linguistic abilities and so on and so on. And linguistic ability gave natural selection . . .

DD:    Sure, obviously we are in accord on that . . .

JE:    Yes, but I want to make it clear that it is language that did it, because there are views to the contrary that are very much expressed. Namely, that

210

language came very late, speaking language, because it had to await the descent of the larynx and the hyoid bone. It was that ordinary human language of even the most primitive kind didn't come until you got *Homo neanderthalis*. How did the brain grow up to *neanderthalis*—it's as big a brain as we have—if it wasn't driven in the biological evolution with the necessity for language?

DD:   There are arterial markings, aren't there, on the skull which suggest big development in Broca–Wernicke's area well back.

JE:   Even that—it has been described by Tobias and Holloway. I accept that in a way, I've said it in my book. But I think just the brain size itself is the important thing, because that is there for all to see. You can do the endocasts of the brain of *Homo habilis* and see this enormous increase.

DD:   It went up 200 cc about then, but it also went up about another 200 cc from *habilis* to *erectus*.

JE:   But this is still more language you see—more language.

DD:   Well, I suppose the point I am making about fire is, not that it caused, per se, the development of language. In a way we don't really know when it came, do we, insofar as the issue of preservation of ashes and everything else in the tropics. I mean the people that have looked at this, I mean it is a rather difficult thing. Ashes wouldn't, under tropical conditions, be likely to be preserved for subsequent scientists.

JE:   The first records, I think, are in China. *Homo erectus* had got through to China, and that was only

500 000 years ago, or something like that.* They had very large brains over 1000 ccs at that time. Of course, what you say could have been relevant to the later development, but the first development up to this level was based upon the necessity for language, which is distinctively human. Other animals have signals of all kinds but they don't describe to one another and they don't argue.

DD:   Well I mean, I suppose what I am proposing is that around that period of time, with the discovery of fire and people gathered at night, there would be a major acceleration factor with language.

JE:   It would help—everything helps you see involving human communication with one another, and these tribal society groups would only be fifty to one hundred at the most. They are not large groups. Of course, this is a hunter–gatherer society. They just can't be big. They'd never get big until we got to the agricultural revolution. That was some 10 000 years ago. The first known settled towns were Jericho and Catal Huyuk.

---

\* There is evidence for earlier use of fire. C.K. Brain and A. Sillen (*Nature* 1 December 1988 vol. 336 pp. 464) describe burnt bones heated to a range of temperatures consistent with that occurring in campfires in deposits in Swartkrans cave dated 1.0–1.5 million years ago, but not in earlier levels. There were 270 pieces of bone judged to be burnt among the 59 488 fossil fragments discovered, mainly antelopes, but also zebra, warthog, baboon and, interestingly, also Australopithicene robustus. The bones were cut marked indicating butchery. Tools were present in all levels, and the authors propose that both Homo and Australopithicenes were present. As the authors state, the data do not necessarily show the fire was used for cooking, protection against predators or the provision of warmth, or it may have been used for all three reasons. It might be construed as adding weight to the light at night argument as conducive to development of language.

DD:   Yes. Well in relation to this very rapid development of the brain and what you've proposed as inexplicable in the evolutionary process—namely, the emergence of the unique sense of self-awareness—you have cited Alfred Russell Wallace, who co-discovered evolution by natural selection with Darwin, as sharing a view on this, and this concerned primitive people. He held that the brain of primitive peoples could not have arrived by natural selection, and that a higher intelligence had intervened. He said, and you noted it outraged Darwin, that natural selection could only have endowed the savage with the brain a little superior to that of an ape. Whereas he actually possesses one a little inferior to that of the average members of our learned societies.

JE:   Nothing exciting in performances . . . good fun, I think.

DD:   Yes, however, if we can look a little further at what Wallace said he noted that brains differed in quality as well as quantity, but stated that the brains of the Teutonic family were 94 cubic inches, and were larger than that of Tasmanians at 82, or Eskimos 91, or Bushmen 77. But in fact, there was not much difference in brain size despite the vast differences in mental capacities of a Cambridge mathematical wrangler and the lowest savage. Wallace's main point was a vast difference in the brain size of apes and that of the lowest savage—yet the lowest savages passed their lives so as to require the exercise of few faculties not possessed in an equal degree by many animals. Now Wallace says that they don't do much except satisfy the cravings of appetite in the simplest and easiest ways. And the large brain of savage man is much beyond his actual requirements in the savage state. He was implying, of course, that they were getting ready for something. Now I am wondering whether you'd actually accept this proposition—though you did cite Wallace. In the light of the contemporary anthropological appreciation of the complex inter-relations and behavioural constraints arising from the hierarchies in primitive societies, and the needs of intelligence to survive and dominate, also there's a continuing development of language and skills with primitive tools and hunting strategies, and often rich and imaginative mythologies of life. The gap to the gorilla and the chimpanzee is actually, you know, enormous, and I wonder whether in fact Wallace is quite wrong on this count?

JE:  Now, what is the point? I think it was this. He was thinking of natural selection as a biological process, and merely stating this with the Indonesians that he was living amongst—he spent very much of his life under these conditions, Darwin never did at all. He was living with them and seeing this against the orangutan, which is the local ape in that area. He felt that difference between them, and why did they need to have this great brain development when the orangutan in the same environment could just about get by with much less brain? It was, of course, naive but Wallace was not a great scholar. He was a wonderful biologist, naturalist, one of the world's greatest, but he did put that up. I keep on asking the same question. What was it that gave to—you mentioned a wrangler, mathematical wrangler—what gave that ability in the natural evolution story, and you can't tell me. You see, because of this, all this higher level we have came only quite recently. There were no great mathematicians two thousand years ago. There were beginnings with Euclid and Ptolemy and so on. But already the brain had fully developed in *Homo sapiens sapiens* 30 000 years ago. And there it was, and the brain was lying there for the richness of eventually creating music. Now, this is no natural selection. You don't survive better with better music. But the brain was made with these immense abilities, abilities for us to discuss these very questions, there's no natural selection in that. Somehow or other in the evolutionary process we went far beyond what was required by any Darwinian evolution, and that's what Wallace's point was. I think he was right in that.

DD:   You mean, it's like Jung said—Columbus, with an erroneous hypothesis, nevertheless discovered America . . . This same argument is discussed by Humphrey in relation to the size of the brain of the gorilla. The gorillas are layabouts, but as he points out they've got very complex societies and hierarchies, and a gorilla has a lot to attend to to look after its own position. It's not just merely a matter of feeding.

JE:   No, that's still trivial compared with the ordinary life we have. You take the primitive man—primitive *Homo sapiens sapiens*. They went on for a long, long time, longer than the civilised *Homo sapiens sapiens*. They were primitive people starting, if you like to believe the modern story now, in Africa 90 000 years ago, with a brain like ours, and the potentiality of ours. And we know that if you take the most primitive people in the world today and adopt their babies and bring them into our society they do quite well—as Gadusek has proved many times. So our brains have developed in some amazing way with potentialities for the future which were not at all related to survival under natural selection. You see, because the human abilities have transcended everything in biology in an incredible way. So that is what my book is partly about. We get into a new world of existence at a higher

215

mental function and creative functions in mathematics and music, to give you two examples, or you can name as many as you like and language as well with all the creative abilities in linguistic usage. So there it is. No one has ever answered that question of Wallace's properly.

DD:   Well, you see another explanation.

JE:   Of course, because . . . explanations, I believe they're all part of the divine plan and this came in the whole evolutionary process. I believe that right through there was some kind of guidance on the way. Divine providence or what you will, but we're not just happening, chance out of chaos as, say, Jacques Monod would have said . . . But he didn't explain himself— that was the point. Jacques Monod explained us but he didn't explain himself!

*The remainder of the discussion has been incorporated into chapter 4.*

* * *

*Dr Donald Griffin*

Dr Donald Griffin, the distinguished experimental naturalist, now works at the Concord Field Station of Harvard University. Soon after his initial studies in biology at Harvard University he began working with George Pierce, professor of physics, and they showed that bats emitted 'supersonic' sounds.

After his work as a graduate student on the homing of birds, which included following them in an aeroplane, he and his collaborators established the use of echo location by bats not only to avoid stationary objects but also for hunting their rapidly moving insect prey. The impact of this discovery—embodying the principle of radar—on the contemporary scientific community is described superbly by Dr Richard Dawkins in his great book *The Blind Watchmaker* (Longman, 1986; Penguin, 1991). From 1965 onwards Griffin carried out comparative behaviour research supported by Rockefeller University and the New York Zoological Society, and it was during the 1970s that his great interest in cognitive processes in animals developed. This led to his important books, *The Question of Animal Awareness* (Rockefeller University Press, 1981) and *Animal Thinking* (Harvard University Press, 1984).

TRANSCRIPT OF A DISCUSSION WITH DR DONALD GRIFFIN, HARVARD, BOSTON, OCTOBER 1990.

DD:   Did your fascination with echo location in bats, and the creatures avoiding obstacles in a flight path when those obstacles had been removed shortly before, lead you to the issue of images and, thus, consciousness in animals?

DG:   Well, I think that may have been one factor. It wasn't a major one I think. But it always was very striking when one had been studying bats' sonar and seeing how well they could detect very small objects to find—and this wasn't an original work with me, the experiments were done by Moehres in Germany—that after they are thoroughly familiar with the flight space they will bump into newly erected obstacles, even great big things like a sheet of plywood. Also they will turn back from where a wall used to be if you removed the wall. So they obviously learned a sort of pattern and are flying on the basis of that memory and ignor-

ing the very strong echoes or the absence of echoes that ordinarily they could use for detecting much smaller things. This I think is a little suggestive that they are perhaps thinking about the space but it wasn't I think a major spur in my developing interest in animal consciousness.

*The next section of discussion has been incorporated into chapter 3.*

DD:   With the birds, what about numeracy, that is, parrots counting?

DG:   Yes, parrots have been shown to, one particular parrot, whom I will call Alex Pepperberg after the scientist, Dr Pepperberg, who had studied him for many years. She has taught him to use his imitation of human speech, in this case, American English, in apparently a rather meaningful way. I will get back to the counting in a minute, but it's part of a larger series of studies that she has made with this one African Grey parrot. He asks for things that he wants using their English names that he has been taught. And if you doubt that he has really asked for the red pasta and give him something else then he squawks and throws it on the floor. Pretty clearly he wanted this one particular thing. These are not food items. These are things that he plays with and Pepperberg has taught him this through a rather complicated procedure called social modelling, where she and another person communicate and show each other things and give their names and the parrot sort of joins in the game and in that way has learned to, as I say, use English words in a meaningful manner. Now, among other things, he can say whether two things are the same or different, and he has learned to say the number of objects shown to him—if he is shown three marbles he will say three, and four marbles, four. But he can generalise to other novel objects different from the ones where he learned to say three when there were three marbles, he will say three for three matchboxes or three of anything else, at least, a wide range of things. There are other experiments: Koehler in Germany taught a raven, many years ago, one or two ravens perhaps, to select from a number of small boxes the one that was marked with a certain number of objects on the surface—rather round blobs I think, but the marks could be quite different from each other. For example, the raven might have learnt that it got food by opening the box with four marks on it, and perhaps the marks were squares originally, but then, given a box with four little discs on it, he would go to that box. This seemed to work up to a number in the order of six or seven but not higher—and there have been other experiments of that general kind. There is argument about them: some scientists say the bird isn't really learning the number, it's learning some kind of a pattern—but it's a pattern that is rather closely related to number. In the case of Alex, the African parrot that Dr Pepperberg has worked with, he actually says two, three or four, so that I think he is telling us that he is thinking two, three or four.

DD: Can they show him, say, two, three or four things on a screen, or something like that, that he can recognise?

DG: I think the experiments have involved actual objects rather than projected images. The experiments that I recall hearing about and reading about did. I think Dr Pepperberg has been trying to get Alex to respond to projected images because you could do quite a few experiments better that way. To my knowledge she has not shown that Alex can recognise numbers of objects when they're projected images, but I may just not be familiar with the details of her experiment.

DD: Well, the great Cambridge, UK, zoologist Thorpe, in accord with what you have been saying, thought there were powerful reasons for concluding that consciousness is a widespread feature of animal life. He cited William James who said consciousness is what we might expect in an organ added for the sake of steering a nervous system grown too complex to regulate itself. Well, in this regard the searchlight of attention, accepting some but rejecting a vast amount of sensory inflow, produces an integrated perception of the present and considers whether it is congruent with the past. But I suppose when there is a consideration of one of several options of action there is the necessity of consciousness and presumptively a great biological advantage attendant on it.

DG: I am not sure it is absolutely necessary but I think it is clearly advantageous, and I would like to borrow a phrase from the philosopher Karl Popper, although he was, I am sure, applying it to human consciousness. It is very advantageous if you can think about the various things you might do and what is likely to happen and try them all out in your head rather than going out in the real world and eating this or going up to that animal and only discovering that the food is bad to eat when it makes you sick, or only discovering that that animal is a predator when he eats you.

DD: You get killed!

DG: That's an inefficient way of doing things, whereas if you can think about it and think, well, that's a big thing like the one that I saw carry off my companion last week, and avoid that animal, this is an advantageous way to use a central nervous system. And it seems to me that it must be advantageous for a wide variety of animals to think consciously in these simple kinds of terms. If I do that I'll probably get hurt or if I go there I will probably get something good to eat. So that this kind of very simple conscious thinking about alternatives may be very widespread and I would think that Popper's arguments about it being an advantage in our species are equally applicable to many other species, although I am not sure whether he would agree with that or not.

DD: Yes, well, one of the arguments is that human thinking is linked to language, which is no doubt true in large measure. But it seems much human thought and fantasy can be non-linguistic in character, and in this regard, you know, may be closer to thought processes in animals. I take it you've said that the belief that mental experiences are the prerogative of one species—'It is not only unparsimonious, it's actually a bit conceited?'

DG:  Yes, it seems so to me. Many scientists and other people do feel that this is a unique human attribute—something that makes us different from and superior to all other living animals. And I would agree that our language is enormously more complex and versatile, and we can think and do all sorts of difficult things that no other species can manage because they don't have the mental capabilities, and particularly the advantage of human language. But it seems to me highly likely that this is not something that appeared all of a sudden in one blinding flash whether a million years ago or some other period of time. Like all other attributes it evolved gradually and that simpler analogs or similar processes probably go on in the central nervous systems of other animals. As you say there is a great deal of human thinking that is not strictly linguistic, and obviously some people can't speak because of impediments, impairment of either the brain or the larynx—but they are obviously thinking, so you have to say it is not the actual speech that is necessary, it's the capability.

DD:  They could be thinking, learnt it earlier.

DG:  They learnt it earlier, and they undoubtedly do but there is a lot of thinking that is not really in words, in fact it is quite difficult to put it into words—that's one of the challenges.

DD:  People have fantasies.

DG:  We have thoughts that aren't easily put into words. Furthermore, it would seem to me, and I am returning to a theme that I have tried to stress, that when animals communicate with each other, some of the time at least, it probably is a process of conveying simple thoughts and there are some examples where we can see at least some of what those thoughts might be. It's not the customary way in which scientists studying animal behaviour have thought about animal communication, but I think perhaps they should.

DD: Yes, well, obviously this issue of language is central. In the case of humans it involves propositions. It's structured if you like, that is, it has a syntax, and it expresses intent. Well, abstract symbolisms, as with language, mathematics and musical notation, are supposedly the apogee of human thought, and on the face of it delineate man from the other creatures and I have no doubt that that's true. But the evidence on symbolic communication in apes is based on teaching American sign language to them and observing that the chimps will initiate communication to get what they want. That seems to be well established, but Terrace's findings with his chimp—Nim Chimpsky—have suggested there is little or no evidence of linguistic communication, in that there is no combinatorial activity, no real syntax. But as I understand it, the work at Yerkes of Savage Rumbaugh and her two chimps, Sherman and Austin, has shown at least a high level of cooperative activity between the two, based on a sign language for mutual benefit.

DG: Yes, that's correct—I don't think Dr Savage Rumbaugh would claim that there is much syntax, if any, but there is a great deal of semantic communication. That is communication of meaning, and quite specific meaning which seems to me to be evidence of thought. If you can communicate something there must be the same information or the simple idea must be in your central nervous system to begin with. Now those particular experiments with the two chimpanzees, Sherman and Austin, were designed primarily to explore how well they could do at communication about a cooperative task. At the Yerkes Laboratory they don't use the American sign language of manual gestures; instead they provide for the chimpanzee a simple computer keyboard.

DD: This is the Washoe experiment with ASL (American Sign Language used by the deaf).

DG: And Terrace, and several others—and that's very significant. But the Sherman and Austin experiments involved a sort of keyboard where there were fairly large, perhaps two inch square lighted keys that the chimpanzee or the human experimenter could touch. There would be several, maybe twenty, thirty or fifty on a keyboard. And the chimpanzees had learned that pressing a certain one was the way you got a certain tool. And they also learned to use tools to get at food that was put in places that required a tool to get it. A key to open a box or, for example, the food might be put in a long transparent tube and the only way to get it was to take a long thin stick and poke it through the tube. So there were five or six or so kinds of food in containers that required five or six different kinds of tools, and both these chimpanzees had learned to get food using these tools, and to ask for the tool by pressing the right key on the keyboard. Then what was arranged was a situation where they were in separate rooms with a window. They could look through at each other, and there was a very small doorway that they could pass tools back and forth or other things, but they were much too small for a chimpanzee to climb through. So then one of them, say, Austin, was put in the room with the food and the container (sorry I didn't explain this fully). The other chimpanzee, in this case Sherman, could not see the food, could not see what the problem was, and Austin had to use his keyboard to ask Sherman—the chimpanzee in the other room—to give him the right tool, and this worked. They did almost perfectly learn to ask for the right tool and the other chimpanzee would pass it through, and then they would share some of the food which is sometimes quite difficult to teach chimpanzees to do.

DD: They have to be taught to share?

DG: They have to be taught to share—and that was apparently almost as difficult as teaching them to ask for tools with a keyboard.

DD: Just like real life!

DG: Savage Rumbaugh and her colleagues have gone on to studying pygmy chimpanzees or bonobos, which have become even more versatile than Sherman and Austin, and use this keyboard in a quite remarkable way. Kanzi, one particular young male pygmy chimpanzee, had been carried about and was quite young, one or two years, with his mother but they were not trying to teach him to use the keyboard. They were trying to teach the mother and she was not doing very well, and after a while they took her away and left Kanzi with the keyboard, and he rushed right over to it and began pressing it and asking for things that he wanted. He'd apparently learned the process just by watching his mother, and by watching the people trying to teach his mother, as they were demonstrating. Well, he's gone on from there and now he uses such a keyboard to ask for places he wants to be taken or ask to be tickled, and he can translate between spoken English words and the keyboard, and so on. So, in general, these chimpanzees at the Yerkes Laboratory seemed to me to have demonstrated a very considerable degree of semantic communication. Not much syntax, if any—on the other hand, I am not sure that they really tried to develop syntax.

There are some other experiments with dolphins, where Louis Herman, the same one I mentioned earlier, has specifically set out to see whether dolphins can learn a simple syntax. He had two dolphins, one of which was trained to recognise underwater sounds, and the other manual gestures of a trainer beside the tank. They were taught a number of signals, meaning that the dolphin should do certain things, such as go to a ball, and there were different signals if it was the red ball or the blue ball. That's not very novel, because similar things, much more complicated things, have been taught to other dolphins, but what Herman set out to do was to teach a simple syntax, which is not the same as English syntax but similar in that the word order, the signal sequence, is important. The first signal might be the thing to go to, the second signal is what you do to it when you get there, and modifiers of colour were put before the object. So, up to about five such signals or words, if you want to call them that, the dolphins could learn. But in doing these experiments Herman very carefully exposed them only to a few out of the many combinations of these signals that were meaningful, and then, after that was done, the crucial part of the experiment was to give them a new sequence—or quote sentence, if you want to call it that. The dolphins did very well at that; they did the right thing even though it was a combination that they had never encountered before. Well, as always in these things, there are scientific sceptics who don't agree with the interpretation of the original experimenter. In this case one of the objections has been that this whole system is so simple that all the dolphins had to learn was two rules and then they could do the whole thing. Well, learning two syntactic rules is better than being unable to learn any syntactic rule, and granted that this is a very simple kind of syntax, apparently dolphins can learn that much of a conveying of meaning by the word order, or the signal order—the temporal arrangement of the signals. That I think is the strongest evidence for anything like syntax in animals so far.

DD:   I wonder what your ideas are on the issue of awareness in animals of their own impending death?

DG:   Yes, that's an interesting question and I really don't have much to say about it. Some people have said that animals have no notion at all that at some time they will die, and of course, if you don't believe an animal has any awareness of itself, it can hardly have an awareness of itself dying!

DD:   No, I'm thinking of the Richter experiment.

DG:   In general this is a question—many people say animals don't have any sort of awareness of their death. Curt Richter, a brilliant physiologist at Johns Hopkins, several years ago did an interesting experiment in which he was studying the reaction of rats that were forced to swim for various lengths of time. I think he probably thought, I would have thought, and most people would have thought, that wild rats trapped in the streets of Baltimore would be much tougher and last much longer in this stressful situation than laboratory white rats, but it turned out the other way around. The wild rats, at least in some experiments, seemed to give up and stop trying to swim much sooner than the laboratory rats did. But he also found, and this is what makes it interesting, that if the rats had been exposed to very brief immersion and then had been rescued or given some way of climbing out, they apparently learned, both the laboratory rats and the wild rats, that this situation wasn't as hopeless as it had seemed. After that experience the wild rats did swim and kept trying much longer than freshly caught wild rats. So this suggests that there was some kind of a feeling of hopelessness in the original rats. They were in this very strange and unfamiliar situation of having to swim and not being able to climb out of the water. It seems likely, or possible, that they just felt that this was hopeless and gave up. Now physiologically that is similar, as you have pointed out, to cases of sudden death without any real injury in other animals and people—it seems to result from over-activity of the vagus nerve, slowing or even stopping the heart. This seemed to be what was going on in these rats also. But the interesting thing from the point of view of animal consciousness is—did these rats actually feel it's hopeless, I'm going to die? I don't think the experiment is enough to demonstrate that they had any idea they were going to die, they certainly gave up—they stopped swimming, their vagus nerves were active, their hearts dilated and they died. It's suggestive but I think not conclusive, and perhaps not even as strongly suggestive as some of these other kinds of evidence that animals might be thinking about things. On the other hand, animals see other animals killed and die all the time. Many species do. And if they have any simple awareness of themselves and of the likely results of certain things it would seem quite plausible that having seen a predator take and kill and eat some of their companions, when they see the same predator rushing at them they might well suppose that this might happen to them, but this is all just speculative. I don't have any direct evidence that bears on it.

DD: Yes, predators themselves of course, in the course of hunting, and hunting as a group, often take evasive action and so on, on the basis, one might guess, that they're avoiding getting hurt.

DG: Yes, when they're attacking dangerous prey like, say, wolves attacking a moose, which can and sometimes does hurt them. They certainly rush in and back off and do all kinds of things to avoid getting hurt. I am not sure how strong the evidence is that they are consciously thinking about getting hurt. They might simply have learned that this is how you attack a moose, but both predators and prey show another kind of behaviour that's sort of suggestive. They both monitor each other in many cases. In Schaller's and Crook's and Walther's studies of predators and prey in East Africa, where you can see them quite well, the gazelles spend a lot of time watching lions and and if the lions don't look as though they are dangerous they go right on feeding but they just move away, they don't let the lion get too close. But once the lion gets set to attack then they notice a difference and rush off to a much greater distance. Likewise, predators notice small details, that human scientists have a hard time noticing, indicating that certain animals are weak or sick or more vulnerable. Kruuk describes how he darted and anaesthetised various animals to mark them and they would recover and they would look perfectly normal to him, but hyenas would rush over and attack them, and they couldn't run very fast. He learned that he had to stand by with his Land Rover and protect these gazelles until they were really fully recovered from the anaesthetic and could run vigorously. So that both predators and prey, and this is true of fish apparently also, are quite adept at watching each other, and noticing small signs of vulnerability in the case of prey, or a tendency of a likelihood of attack in the case of a predator. You would think they might be thinking a little bit about it—that lion, he is safe, he is not going to come at me, but that lion looks as though he might come—I had better watch out. That kind of simple thinking, conscious thinking, seems to me, at least, plausible, although, as always, you can't absolutely prove it.

*The remainder of the discussion has been incorporated into chapter 3.*

# Bibliography and further reading

Books and articles that served as main references in preparation of these chapters

ADRIAN, E.D. 'Consciousness', in J.C. Eccles (ed.) *Brain and Conscious Experience*, Springer Verlag, Berlin, 1966

AMSTERDAM B. 'Mirror Self-image Reactions before aged 2', *Developmental Psychobiology* 5: p. 297, 1972

BAUDELAIRE, C. *Flowers of Evil*, New Directions, New York, 1958

BERLIN, I. *The Crooked Timber of Humanity: Chapters in the History of Ideas*, John Murray, London, 1990

BLAKEMORE, C. *The Mind Machine*, BBC Classic Books, London, 1983

BOWRA, C.M. *The Greek Experience*, Mentor Books, New York, 1957

BREUIL, Abbé H. *Four Hundred Centuries of Cave Art*, Centre d'Etudes et de Documentation Prehistoriques, Montignac, Dordogne

CAMPBELL, J. *Primitive Mythology: The Masks of God*, Penguin Books, 1976

—— *The Way of Animal Powers*, Historical Atlas of World Mythology, Time Books, London, 1984

CAPRA, F. *The Turning Point: Science, Society and the Rising Culture*, Bantam Books, London, 1983

CHANGEAUX, J-P. *Neuronal Man: The Biology of Mind*, Oxford University Press, Oxford, 1985

CRICK, F.H.C. *Thinking about the Brain: In the Brain*, A Scientific American book, W.H. Freeman & Co., San Francisco, 1979

—— *What Mad Pursuit*, Penguin Books, London, 1988

CROOK, J.H. *The Evolution of Human Consciousness*, Clarendon Press, Oxford, 1980

DAWKINS, R. *The Blind Watchmaker*, Longman, London, 1986

DENTON, D. *The Hunger for Salt*, Springer Verlag, Berlin/London, 1982

DESMOND, A. *The Ape's Reflexion*, Blond & Briggs, London, 1979

DODDS, E.R. *The Greeks and the Irrational*, University of California Press, Berkeley, 1951

ECCLES, J.C. (ed.) *Brain and Conscious Experience*, Study Week of the Pontifical Academy of Science, Springer Verlag, Berlin, 1966

—— 'Animal Consciousness and Human Self-consciousness', *Experientia* 38: p. 1384, 1982

—— *The Evolution of the Brain: Creation of the Self*, Routledge, London, 1989

—— 'Language, Thought and Brain', *Epistemologica* 4: special issue, p. 97, 1981

—— 'A Unitary Hypothesis of Mind–Brain Interaction in the Cerebral Cortex', *Proc. R. Soc. Lond.* 240: p. 433, 1990

EDELMAN, G.M. *Neural Darwinism: The Theory of Neuronal Group Selection*, Oxford University Press, Oxford, 1989

ELDREDGE, N. and GOULD, S.J. 'Punctuated Equilibria: An Alternative to Phyletic Gradualism', in T.J.M. Schopf (ed.) *Models of Paleobiology*, Freeman Copper, San Francisco, 1972

FERNAND, W. *Lascaux*, Centre des Etudes et de Documentation Dordogne, 1948

FITZSIMONS, J.T. *The Physiology of Thirst and Sodium Appetite*, Cambridge University Press, Cambridge, 1979

GALLUP, G.G. Jnr 'Towards an Operational Definition of Self-awareness', in R.H. Tuttle (ed.) *Socio-Ecology and Psychology of Primates*, The Hague, Mouton, 1975

—— 'Self-recognition in Primates: A Comparative Approach to the Bidirectional Properties of Consciousness, *American Psychologist* p. 329, May 1977

GAZZANIGA, M.S. *The Social Brain: Discovering the Networks of the Mind*, Basic Books, New York, 1985

GOULD, S.J. *Ever Since Darwin: Reflections on Natural History*, Penguin Books, London, 1977

GREGORY, R.L. *The Oxford Companion to the Mind*, Oxford University Press, Oxford, 1987

GRIFFIN, D.R. *The Question of Animal Awareness: Evolutionary Continuity of Mental Experience*, Wm Kaufmann Inc., Los Altos, Calif., 1981

—— *Animal Thinking*, Harvard University Press, Cambridge, Mass., 1984

HESS, W.R. *The Biology of Mind*, University of Chicago Press, Chicago, 1964

HUMPHREY, N. *The Inner Eye*, Faber & Faber, London, 1986

JOHN, E. and THATCHER, R.W. 'Neurophysiology of Arousal and Attention. Foundations of Cognitive Processes', *Functional Neuroscience*, vol. 1, L. Erlbaum Assoc., New Jersey, 1977

KAHN, C.H. 'Sensation and Consciousness in Aristotle's Psychology', in J. Barnes, M. Schofield and R. Sorabji (eds) *Articles on Aristotle, Psychology and Aesthetics*, Duckworth, London, 1979

KAWABATA, Y. 'Japan, the Beautiful and Myself', Nobel lecture, Les Prix Nobel, The Nobel Foundation, 1968

KENNY, A.J.P., LONGUET-HIGGINS, H.C., LUCAS, J.R. and WADDINGTON, C.H. *The Nature of Mind*, Edinburgh University Press, Edinburgh, 1973

LLOYD, G.E.R. *Aristotle—The Growth and Structure of his Thought*, Cambridge University Press, Cambridge, 1968

—— *Greek Science After Aristotle*, Chatto & Windus, London 1973

—— *Early Greek Science: Thales to Aristotle*, Chatto & Windus, London

LOVELOCK, J.E. *Gaia—A New Look at Life on Earth*, Norton, New York, 1988

LUMDSDEN, C. and WILSON, E.O. *Promethean Fire: Reflec-*

*tions on the Origin of Mind*, Harvard University Press, Cambridge, Mass., 1983

MARLER, P. 'Song-learning Behaviour: The Interface with Neuroethology, *Trends in Neurological Sciences* 14: p. 199, 1991

MARSHALL, A.J. *Bower Birds: Their Displays and Breeding Cycles*, Clarendon Press, Oxford, 1954

MAY, M.T. *Galen—On the Usefulness of Parts of the Body*, Cornell University Press, Ithaca, 1968

MONTAIGNE, *Essays*, Everymans Library, J.M. Dent & Sons, London, 1910

MUKHAMETOV, L. 'Uni-hemispheric Slow Wave Sleep in the Brain of Dolphins and Seals', in *Endogenous Sleep Substances and Sleep Regulation*, p. 67, V.N.U. Science Press, Utrecht, 1985

NERUDA, P. 'Towards the Splendid City', Nobel Lecture in Literature, Les Prix Nobel, The Nobel Foundation, 1971

NIETZSCHE, F. *The Gay Science*, Random House, New York, 1974

NOTTEBOHM, F. 'Reassessing the Mechanisms and Origins of Vocal Learning in Birds', *Trends in Neurological Sciences* 14: p. 206, 1991

OJEMANN, G.A. 'Cortical Organisation of Language', *Journal of Neuroscience* 11: p. 2281, 1991

PARADIS, M. 'Bilingualism and Aphasia', *Stud. Neurolinguistics* 3: p. 65, 1977

PENFIELD, W. 'Speech, Perception and the Uncommitted Cortex', in J.C. Eccles (ed.) *Brain and Conscious Experience*, Springer Verlag, Berlin, 1966

PENFIELD, W. and PEROT, P. 'The Brain's Record of Auditory and Visual Experience', *Brain* 86: p. 595, 1963

PIZZEY, G. *Animals and Birds in Australia*, Cassell Australia, 1966

PLUM, F. and VOLPE, B.T. 'Neuroscience and Higher Brain Function: From Myth to Public Responsibility', in *The Hand Book of Physiology: The Nervous System* 5, American Physiological Society, Washington, D.C., 1987

POPPER, K.R. and ECCLES, J.C. *The Self and its Brain*, Springer Verlag, 1977

PROUST, M. *Remembrance of Things Past*, translated by C.K. Scott Moncrieff and Terence Kilmartin, Penguin Books, London, 1983

RESTAK, R. *The Brain*, Bantam Books, Toronto/New York, 1984

—— *The Mind*, Bantam Books, Toronto/New York, 1988

ROSE, S.P.R. *The Conscious Brain*, Weidenfeld & Nicholson, London, 1973

ROSS, D. *Aristotle. Parva Naturalia: A Commentary*, Clarendon Press, Oxford, 1965

RUSSELL, Bertrand, *Wisdom of the West*, Crescent Books, London, 1959

SOLZHENITSYN, A. Nobel lecture in Literature, Les Prix Nobel, The Nobel Foundation, 1976

SPERRY, R.W. 'Mind–Brain Interaction: Mentalism, yes; Dualism, no', *Neuroscience* 5: p. 195, 1980

TERRACE, H.S. *Nim*, Alfred A. Knoff, New York, 1979

THOMAS, L. *The Medusa and the Snail*, Viking Press, New York, 1974

—— in Clifton Fadiman (ed.) *Living Philosophies*, Doubleday, New York, 1990

THORPE, W.H. 'Ethology and Consciousness', in J.C. Eccles (ed.) *Brain and Conscious Experience*, Springer Verlag, Berlin, 1966

TREVARTHEN, C. 'Split-brain and the Mind' in *The Oxford Companion to the Mind*, Oxford University Press, Oxford, 1987

VINCE, M.A., ARMITAGE, S.E., BALDWIN, B.A., TONER, J. and MOORE, B.C.J. 'The Sound Environment of the Fetal Sheep', *Behaviour* 81: p. 296, 1982

WALKER, S. *Animal Thought*, Routledge & Kegan Paul, London, 1983

WEISKRANTZ, L. (ed.) 'Animal Intelligence: A Discussion', *Philos. Trans. R. Society (London)* 308: pp. 1–216, 1985

WELLS, H.G., HUXLEY, J. and WELLS, G. P. *The Science of Life: A Summary of Contemporary Knowledge about Life and its Possibilities*, 3 vols, Amalgamated Press, London

WILSON, E.O. *Biophilia*, Harvard University Press, Cambridge, Mass., 1984

WILSON, E.O. 'On Naturalism in Living Philosophies', in Clifton Fadiman (ed.) *Living Philosophies*, Doubleday, New York, 1990

WINSTON, J. 'The Meaning of Dreams', *Scientific American*, p. 42, November 1990

WOOLF, V. *The Common Reader*, Hogarth Press, London, 1968

WORDSWORTH, W. 'Lines written above Tintern Abbey', in *Lyrical Ballads*, vol. 1, K. Longman & O. Rees, London, 1800

YOUNG, J.Z. *Philosophy and the Brain*, Oxford University Press, Oxford, 1986

—— 'A change of mind', *Nature* 344: p. 117, 1990

During the proof stage of this book, the following four texts of very great interest have been published:

DENNETT, D.C. *Consciousness Explained*, Allen Lane, The Penguin Press, London, 1992

DIAMOND, J. *The rise and fall of the third chimpanzee*, Vintage, London, 1992

EDELMAN, J. *Bright air, brilliant fire*, Allen Lane, The Penguin Press, London, 1992

HUMPHREY, N. *A history of the mind*, Chatto & Windus, London, 1992

# Index